Power

of

Aleph Beth

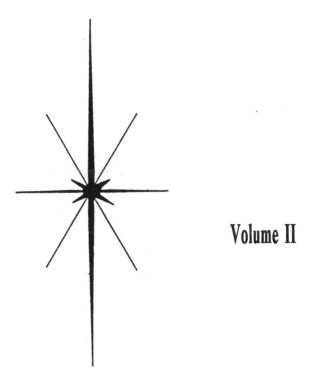

Volume II

RESEARCH CENTRE OF KABBALAH PRESS
JERUSALEM — NEW YORK

POWER
of
ALEPH BETH

by

DR. PHILIP S. BERG

FIRST EDITION
February 1988

ISBN 0-943688-56-6 (Hardcover)
0-943688-57-4 (Softcover)

For further information, address:
RESEARCH CENTRE OF KABBALAH
200 PARK AVENUE, SUITE 303E
NEW YORK, N.Y. 10017
—OR—
RESEARCH CENTRE OF KABBALAH
P.O.BOX 14168
THE OLD CITY, JERUSALEM
ISRAEL

PRINTED IN U.S.A.

THE PUBLICATION OF THIS VOLUME
HAS BEEN MADE POSSIBLE THROUGH
THE SUPPORT OF

ARNOLD E. PRINCE

AND IS DEDICATED TO THE
MEMORY OF HIS FATHER

SOL PRINCE

Table of Contents

Anti-matter; Past Present and Future; The Galaxies; Midat Ha'Din and Midal Ha'Rahamin; Bread of Shame; Interpretation of Teshuvah; Am Segula; The Milky Way; Anti-matter of Eden; Atomic Harmony; Age of Aquarius; Dinosaurs turning into Lizards.

Rotating Satellites; Pre-Fall Of Adam; Quantum Theory; Religion as a Myth; Creator's Withdrawal; Joseph and the Holy Covenant; Central Column; Spanish Expulsion; Converted and Non-Converted; The Jew and His Short Memory; Love Thy Neighbor; The Concept; What is the Word Goy; Nabal's Evil Tongue and David; Tikune Process; Good and Evil and the Erev Rav; Adam and the Souls of Humanity; Noahide Laws; General of the Dor Deah; Gematria; Tower of Babel; Ninth of Av; Sciatic Nerve and Jacob; Raw energy; Herbs and Healing; Adam and Eve; Twenty-Two Intelligent energies; Transpermia.

G'mar Ha'Tikune; Zayin the Shabbath; Force of Tranquility; Manna; Seven Sfirot; Reacting Negativity; Stress.

Letter energies; Human Psyche; Animosity and

ACKNOWLEDGEMENT

I would like to express my gratitude to Kenneth L. Clark, who patiently edited, criticized and reviewed the manuscript.

He made fundamental and frequent contribuitions to the essential ideas and their connection to the overall style. The light I found in our many discussions is one of my principal rewards from this book.

— Dr. Philip S. Berg
November, 1987
New York City

Preface

Can we really learn to control our internal processes with our minds instead of with pills or a soothing glass of something-on-the-rocks? I believe that until such time as each of us comes to grips with the realization that there is a component to life other than the needs of the physical body, we shall, be forced to endure the whims of a life of uncertainty.

The Zohar is designed for people of all ages whose imaginations have not been stifled by the standard Cartesian educational process. It is written for people who are not afraid to embrace "new" ideas, even though these ideas may be a thousand or more years old.

We live in an extraordinary age. All of us must wonder from time to time if there is any real purpose to life. We all have immediate goals, to achieve some gratification in our work, to bring up our offspring. But what of a long-range purpose?

There were a number of themes woven through the structure of Volume I. I thought it might be useful — or at least interesting — to examine the nature of the universe and our role in it, and to explore more closely how the doctrines of the Bible compare with or run contra to the dictates of science.

The range of topics may seem diverse — from the extinction of the dinosaurs to the structure of the cosmos — but, as I hope will emerge, these topics reflect the essence of the Bible, the cosmic code of reality, and provide an overview of the cosmic origins of nature and of man.

Volume II answers many vexing questions concerning destiny, fate and free will. Within the forthcoming chapters, the reader will be given the opportunity of entering a dimension of reality in which he will no longer be an unfortunate victim of circumstances, but rather the creator of his own destiny.

If man is to emerge as more than a mere link in the cosmic chain of uncertainty, we shall need to dispense entirely with the illusion that poses as reality in the physical world.

Kabbalah is meant to make us free. It can give us wings with which to explore the world. And it can free us in a more mundane way, by alerting us to our unique personal challenges and by providing us with the conceptual tools with which to overcome them. When given these potential benefits, we no longer are encouraged to leap of cliffs when our wings are flimsy.

The astronaut suspended between earth and moon sees the earth as it truly is, small and blue and beautiful in the eternal silence where it floats. As the astronaut passes from sunlight into darkness and back again every hour, he or she must become startlingly aware of how artificial are the boundaries we've created to separate and define ourselves.

So here we are, with our backs pressed against the bomb,and our eyes fixed on the stars, in a dilemma that becomes increasingly terrifying. Will we have the wisdom and courage to accept the individual moral reality within each of us? Or will we defer to the illusionary, corporeal reality in the false belief that therein lies our vision of the human future?

How well we answer these questions may have a profound effect on the outcome of this greatest of all experiments called life.

And so, my dear reader,read on

The Author

New York, 1987

The Letter Kaf

כל

Do you know the ordinances of the heavens?
Can you establish their role on Earth?

— Job, 38:33

THE LETTERS WERE GOOD AT UNDERSTANDING THE WORLD. They were searching for their place in the cosmos, but if they were to deal with the cosmos, they were compelled first to ask questions such as: Who are we? What is our internal energy-intelligence? Where are we in this vast expanse of the cosmos?

When cosmic Mem retreated from the stage of creation along with cosmic Lamed and Kaf, cosmic Kaf took a most radical, daring step, unprecedented in the Lord's kingdom.

"At the moment of cosmic Mem's departure, the letter Kaf descended from her throne of glory and returned to the arena of creation. Trembling, she declared, "O Lord of the universe, may it please Thee to commence the art of creation through me. I am the first letter and initial energy-intelligence of thy Kavod, your Honor." Simultaneous with cosmic Kaf's revolutionary action in leaving her Throne, the Throne trembled and, "...two hundred thousand galaxies were about to collapse and fall into ruins.[1]

"Similar catastrophic events are recorded in the scriptures. "The Earth trembled, and the Heavens dropped,"[2] records the Prophetess Deborah in the *Song of Deborah*."The Earth shook, the Heavens also dropped at the presence of the Lord, Even Sinai was moved," declares the psalmist.[3] Various sources of many nations describe catastrophic upheaval and celestial worlds in collision. To quote Job, who describes the cosmic catastrophe at the end of a galactic age: "...which removeth the mountains, which overturneth them in his anger, which shaketh the Earth out of her place..."[4]

We could follow a path around the universe and observe the natural upheavals, some of which were of greater extent and some of lesser import. Kaf's descent from the Lord's throne almost brought to an end the whole of celestial harmony in one sweep.

Most of us never will personally encounter a natural upheaval more violent than a hurricane or an earthquake. Yet with one single activity, cosmic Kaf may have achieved the dubious distinction of creating a disaster involving some two hundred thousand galaxies. Indeed, nothing of this magnitude ever has been recorded. It is an unthinkable event, although the *Zohar* states its possibility.

This reappearance of Kaf in the creative process brings up several closely related problems which briefly must be discussed. The first point is the reason cosmic Kaf ignored the response of the Lord. She had been told that her significant part in the construct of the Throne, was the link which brought together the Lord with His Kingdom. We have examined the three fundamental principles that may be said to govern the cosmic position and general view of the Kaf, but for whatever reason, this, by no means, brought the matter to an end. Cosmic Kaf did not shrink back from her daring suggestion in the matter of her suitability as the channel for the purpose of creation. She did not exercise restraint. She was determined to carry her plea as far as possible.

Are the pleas, with which the letters presented to the Lord concerning their fitness for use in the Creation, merely a sort of interesting cosmic dialogue, or do they represent a dynamic interchange of rhythmically moving cosmos? It is central to the Lord's Force, or Light of Wisdom, to manifest itself in myriad forms. In kabbalistic teachings, the power of thought and words is seen as a cosmic process in which the Force or ultimate reality becomes cosmically expressed.[5] The universe observed through our powerful telescopes is seen in terms of movement and change. An obvious question to be asked about the dynamics of the universe is how and why is this cosmic web motivated? What are its distinguishing features? What are the forces between them?

This observation, however, carries us still deeper into the problem of the plea itself. In what seems to be an apparent attempt by each letter to be considered suitable as the channel for creation over and above their companion letters, their unique importance seems to penetrate and to imply a much deeper cosmic significance than the mere attribute that accompanied each plea.

The plea each letter presented in the creation of the world is similar to the labor involved in setting in motion the cosmic energy-intelligence of *Myin Nukvin* (female waters) in return for *Myin Duhrin* (male waters). The cosmic Force of the Lord, the all embracing unity (*Myin Duhrin*) which provides the essential life-energy-force, depends upon the dimensions of the channel expressing the Force. The letters themselves are the vehicles for *Myin Duhrin*. Their pleas were the consciousness that creates the structure reality of the vessel, the letter.[6]

The concepts prevailing in the new age of physics seem, at first, strange to the Western understanding of things. We have sometimes become confused at the prospect of notions that literally may exist beyond space and time. But what is more striking than all of these strange and startling ideas is the fact that they are not new concepts. Indeed, anyone exploring the pages of kabbalistic material comes away impressed by the unavoidable conclusion that much of the "new" information emerging today has been known for centuries. There are so many parallel concepts between the teachings of the kabbalist and the contemporary scientist that one almost finds it almost impossible to distinguish who said what.

In the past, Newton's universe was constructed from a set of basic "building blocks." The world view suggested by modern physics repeatedly indicates that this idea no longer is tenable. The new philosophy that emerged presented the universe as a dynamic web of interconnected events, an indivisible universe in which all things participate. Everything

in the universe is connected to everything else and no part of
it is fundamental. In a universe which is an inseparable
whole, there is no room for any permanent, fundamental
entity. Even that of human consciousness participates in the
cosmic whole. Kabbalistic teachings have always regarded
consciousness as an integral part of the universe. In the
kabbalistic world view, human beings, like all other life
forms, are bound up with and part of an indivisible cosmic
whole.[7] Therefore, their intelligence implies that the cosmos,
too, is intelligent.

In the words of the renowned kabbalist, R. Yehuda
Ashlag, "The whole of the reality-structuring system of
creation owes its existence to thought consciousness."[8] The
new physics suggests that consciousness itself enters into the
workings of the physically expressed world and determines
it.[9] The full implication of this realization, is of late,
beginning to make itself heard in the scientific community.
Sir James Jeans expressed just this assumption when he wrote,
"The universe begins to look more like a great thought than
like a machine. Mind no longer appears as an accidental
intruder into the realm of matter."[10]

The crucial feature of the plea formulated by the letters
is that the consciousness is not only a necessary part of the
cosmic whole, but is the clue to understanding, determining,
and controlling the reality structure. This is a most important
point in Jewish mysticism. The letters are motivated by the
consciousness. In fact, whether they do or do not exist, how
they become manifest, the degree of their power, rests
entirely on and is bound up with consciousness.

In Jewish mysticism, this universal interrelationship
always includes the human observer and his consciousness, the

plea itself, according to Kabbalah, is that which creates. The plea is the reality that lies beyond physical matter. It encompassed all possible realities. The letters themselves presented a positive structure of reality. This plea in kabbalistic language is termed *Myin Nukvin*. Through the use of mythical language, they meant to decipher the cosmic code of our universe.

Myin Nukvin is the consciousness that originates within the vessel, the receptacle. This feminine polarity, states the *Zohar*, determines the extent and degree that the Force or all embracing unity becomes manifest. "There can be no arousal from above (*Myin Duhrin*) unless there is an arousal from below (*Myin Nukvin*)."[11]

Therefore, the response of the Lord to each letter of the twenty-two letters of *Ze'ir Anpin* and Malkhuth was in the construct of *Myin Duhrin*, the internal consciousness of the Force. The Force began to become manifest as the level of consciousness of each letter. The response, the revelation of the globe of light of the Force, is intrinsically an interplay between *Myin Duhrin* and *Myin Nukvin*. The plea and the response are not only active in the sense of determining the art of creation. They, themselves, are the process.

The claim of the letters before the Lord, to the effect that each one of them deemed herself an acceptable vessel for the purpose of creation, is analogous to the process involved in the dynamic interplay of *Myin Duhrin* and *Myin Nukvin*. This interplay permits *Ze'ir Anpin* and Malkhuth, the channels for the manifestation of the all embracing unity, to bestow Light upon our world. By the utilization of a given letter's dimension of *Myin Duhrin*, the bestowal of Light, depending on the letter, becomes expressed.

The Force of the Lord began to reveal its ruling power, triggered by the plea of the particular letter. Inherent in its revelation was the Lord's response to the particular letter. At the same time, the letter's inadequate power to govern the world would be disclosed. As the effectual battle station of the Lord's kingdom, she could withstand the powerful Death Star fleet. The success or failure of the letters depended entirely on their ability to contain the Lord's all embracing reality. Her failure to withstand an onslaught by the Dark Lord's fleet would be the direct result of the insufficiency of the letter's dimension of light. Just what does this mean?

The ultimate objective of creation was to provide human control over individual destiny. From the kabbalistic view of our universe, there is no conflict between determinism and free will. The constellation of the Death Star was pitted against the structure of the Lord's fleet of *Kedusha*. "The Lord created one against the other,"[12] declares King Solomon. There existed the necessity for room in the deterministic predictive laws of the cosmos for free will.

Solomon appears to offer humankind a unique ability to interprenetrate and influence the structural reality of the universe in a way undreamed of in the days of Newton. Furthermore, the centrality of human beings within the cosmic whole just about demolishes the whole idea of causality and forces us to address the problem of sequence. The concept of universal time with an absolute past, present, and future comes into question. From a kabbalistic point of view, the possibility that an effect may precede its cause is something very real. "There is no past or future in the Bible.[13] The historical presentation of the Bible is not one of sequence."

The sequence of the *sfirot* demonstrates an indeterministic universe. *Sfirot Yesod*, symbolized and portrayed in the Bible as Joseph, precedes in time the birth of Moses, Aaron, and David.[14] However, in its *sfirotic* sequence, the aspect of cause and effect, Yesod follows Netzah and Hod, represented by Moses and Aaron respectively. Does the collapse of determinism conflict with an orderly structured cosmos? If there is no universal present, and the entire future, together with its past, are considered as existing within an indivisible whole, does this mean that footprints seen yesterday on a beach were made today? Do the footprints come before the walker?

It is not the purpose of this book to examine the kabbalistic concept of time. This subject is dealt with elsewhere. What is important here is the revelation of King Solomon. An orderly cosmic structure, the objective of the Lord's dialogue with the letters, does not conflict with the concept of free will. All that the dialogue between the Lord and the letters accomplished was to provide a universe which would prevent the Death Star from seizing control. The Dark Lord's influence would be deeply felt, but never to a point of complete domination.

However, a letter incapable of containing the necessary dimensions of the Force could not maintain a balanced, harmonious universe. The Lord, in pointing to the negative aspect of a letter, was the causal factor for each of the letters to depart and return to its place. Its negative energy-intelligence was the wavelength needed by the Dark Lord to connect and seize control of the letter in its entirety and thereby wrest control of the universe away from the kingdom of the Lord. Therefore, these letters were compelled to depart from the stage of creation.

A letter that was capable of maintaining a sufficient capacity of the Lord's energy-intelligence could resist a final onslaught by the Death Star fleet. Through the process of the dialogue, the letters themselves became aware of who should really be chosen as the proper vessel for use in the creation of the world.

The interpenetration and interconnectedness of the three letters, Mem, Lamed, and Kaf of the word *Melekh* (king), permitted the King, cosmic *Ze'ir Anpin*, to become revealed through cosmic Malkhuth. Thus, the Force of the Lord became manifest within the universe. However, when the energy-intelligence of Mem became revealed, meaning she entered her plea to the Lord, the interconnectedness and interrelationship ended. Kaf terminated her function as security shield and thus descended from the throne of Glory. Her stretched-out version as final Kaf, linking the upper and lower realms of the cosmos, thus came to an end.

This is precisely why the *Zohar* makes no mention of Kaf's appearance and plea, "May it please Thee..." as it did of the other letters. Kaf was moved to approach the Lord only after the revelation of Mem's dimension of her energy-intelligence, or when she entered her plea. The interpenetration between these three cosmic entities was unique. They were strongly and permanently bound up with each other.

Consequently, when cosmic Mem became the dominating power within the cosmos, cosmic Kaf, too, was drawn away from her position at the Throne and descended along with the Mem into the lower celestial realm of our universe. Cosmic Kaf's station, similar to the other letters, is located within the cosmic realm of Briah (Creation). There, individual and collective DNA become established and subsequently become physically expressed in the terrestrial and celestial realms of our universe. Briah provides the life giving force for all universes below.

"When cosmic Kaf stepped down from the throne, she trembled, along with two hundred thousand galaxies." The binding link between celestial realm of Hokhmah and Binah and the lower worlds is Malkhuth. Malkhuth portrays the intermediary force in the cosmos. As the final *sfirah*, or cosmic force in any creative frame of reference, she combines the sole responsibility for any celestial or terrestrial entity becoming manifest. This might be compared to the seed of the fruit which becomes physically expressed at the final stage of development. Nevertheless, the seed becomes the *Keter* (crown), or origin of the subsequent tree.

Kaf maintained the continuity and interconnectedness between the two hundred thousand galaxies and the Force or the Lord's energy-intelligence. The shape of the stretched-out Kaf indicated and provided this cosmic bond. Thus, when the Kaf left her position as Malkhuth of cosmic Briah, she caused a severance in continuity, causing an interruption of the life giving Force to the lower, two-hundred-thousand-galaxy world. They were undergoing a calamity of strangulation. The umbilical cord of the cosmos was threatened.

Elaborating on the concept of the mystical doctrine of the Throne — heretofore one of the most shrouded mysteries of the whole idea of the cosmos — R. Ashlag provides the step-by-step evolutionary process of the celestial realm.[15]

"The Throne has three phases which encompass the whole array of the cosmic realm. The totality of the Lord's energy-intelligence, also referred to as the Force, is based within the upper realm of the cosmos known by the code name *Atziluth*. The Force itself has a code name, *Hochmah*. When the Force is transformed to a lower level referred to as the cosmic realm of *Briah*, the Force itself takes on a new coded designation, *Binah*.

The upper section of the Throne contains six *sfirotic* energy-intelligences, indicated by the four sides of the seat along with the seat itself and the space above the seat. They represent the six cosmic channels of the lower worlds, known as *Hesed*, *G'vurah*, *Tifereth*, *Netzah*, *Hod*, and *Yesod*. The second aspect of the Throne is its four legs which are the *Mohin*, or the energy-intelligence itself, referred to as the brain. (This might be compared to the head of a man wherein the brain, or energy, is stored. The body of man is the vehicle by which the brain becomes manifest). This source of all cosmic channels is known by the coded names, *Keter*, *Hochmah*, *Binah*, and *Daath* of the lower worlds. Third is *Malkhuth* of the immediate upper celestial realm which descends to the next world below, establishing the connection and continuity.

When cosmic Kaf descended from the Throne of Glory — the celestial realm of *Briah* — the connection with the celestial realm of Atziluth became severed. Kaf itself in the process suffered the loss of her energy-intelligence, and "she too trembled." When cosmic Kaf experienced her loss at the Lord's battle station known as *Atziluth*, all subsequent connecting Kaf channels suffered this same deprivation.

Following this traumatic crisis, all two hundred thousand worlds were in need of energy-intelligence which stems from *Atziluth*. They trembled and were about to fall into ruins. The worlds of *Briah*, *Yetzirah*, and *Assiah* came close to annihilation at the hands of the Death Star fleet because the worlds did not contain sufficient Light of the Force to withstand the Dark Lord's assault that was homing in for the final kill.

Consequently, the descent of cosmic Kaf coincided with the retort of the Lord, "Return to the Throne. As a result of your transfer, *Kilyah* (extermination) would be the lot of the worlds. For this reason, you are the first letter and the initiator of the cosmic force of destruction.[16] Your obligation to survive is owed not just to yourself, but also to the cosmos, from which shall ultimately spring mankind.

Her channel was too important in maintaining the harmony and interconnectedness of the vast cosmos. Thus, after the dialogue between the Lord and cosmic Kaf, the Kaf departed to her significant position in the Lord's Throne of Glory.

16

The Letter Yood

There is no excellence among the creatures which is not to be found in a much higher style, and as an archetype, in the Creator; among created beings it exists only in footmarks and images.

— Albertus Magnus

STANDING AT THE LAST DIALOGUE BETWEEN THE LETTERS and a clear view of creation, cosmic Yood was speculating on what lies beyond. The plea of each letter injected an energy-intelligence of *Myin Nukvin*, the Returning Light,[1] into the cosmos. These pulsating pockets of energy would create symmetry within the universe. Known in the lexicon of Kabbalah as the intelligent energy-force of restriction, the central column — the desire to receive for the sake of imparting — this infinite energy became incorporated within the Lord's cosmic production.

In a modern sense, these pockets of energy-intelligence can be referred to as anti-matter. It is the mirror image — the perfectly symmetrical counterpart — of ordinary matter. Matter is governed by the energy-intelligence, or thought force, of the "desire to receive for oneself alone." The positive activity of future man on the terrestrial realm would trigger the energy-intelligence of cosmic *Myin Nukvin*. The response to this activity is the Lord's energy-intelligence, *Myin Duhrin*, the Force, becoming manifest and revealed.

The problem, nevertheless, was to secure the existence and expression of *Myin Nukvin*. This depended entirely upon humankind's positive framework and activity, and from the looks of things, man was going to have a hard time keeping his head above water, let alone being concerned with the welfare of the cosmos. Little would he realize that cosmological influences were going to determine the condition of life on planet Earth.

Yood and the other letters were fearful of the advantage that the Death Star fleet appeared to have over corporeal man and his physical universe. Increasing negative activity by humankind played right into the hands of the Dark Lord. Egocentricity, self-centeredness, and selfishness, were precisely the necessary energy-intelligences required to maintain the Death Star fleet. The Dark Lord played his cards well. Humankind's insatiable desire for momentary pleasure thwarted any counter-offensive that *Myin Nukvin* and the Lord's fleet may have contemplated. *Myin Duhrin* retreated to the Lord's battle station wondering whether mankind would ever activate sufficient *Myin Nukvin* to repulse the Death Star fleet. To vaporize and permanently remove the Darth Vaders from the cosmos, at that time, was but a dreamer's hope for the future.

Has the universe always existed in its observable form? Did the Big Bang[2] represent the beginning of cosmic history? How many other incarnations of the universe were there in the remote past? Can we be sure whether the galaxies are typical of all cosmic epochs? Fortunately, we do have some information, limited though it seems, about what might have occurred back in the depths of cosmic time.

For the kabbalist, it is a simple matter to explore backward in time, making use of the *Book of Formation* and the *Zohar*. The scientist has not the slightest idea whether or not infinitely older cosmos preceded the presently observed universe. Nor can he ascertain whether other galaxies are made of matter or anti-matter. While some interesting theories have been advanced to explain how matter and anti-matter might be separated, there exists no convincing mechanism for detection. The kabbalist, however, is convinced that at one time the two existed as one, for the *Zohar*[3] and the *Midrash*[4] postulate, with striking clarity, a general scenario which takes into account a two stage cosmos, which seems to imply that for an infinite time the universe behaved one way and then abruptly changed to another. Before tackling the central question of whether the universe has altered its governing laws, it is important to assess what the *Zohar* has to say on the subject of primeval epochs.

"In the beginning, before the energy-intelligences were created (long before the formation of the physical universes), the Lord first thought to create the intelligent energies with *Midat Ha'Din* (strict judgment). However, further interpenetration of these energy-intelligences brought the realization that they had no chance of survival once corporeal man made his appearance. Hence, the Lord combined the interconnected *Midat Ha'Rahamim* (compassion) with *Midat Ha'Din*."

Rabbi Ashlag explores the startling revelation of creation by raising the all important question, "Are we to assume that the Lord's thought process is similar to ours?" We mortals tend to change our minds as we gain further insight and experiences of matters that unfold in the future. The Lord's thinking process, however, is not limited by or bound up with time. Past, present, and future are all contained within the source.[5] For corporeal man is there a temptation to assume that only the present really exists.

"However," continues R. Ashlag, "when discussing the relationship of cause and effect, as pertaining to emanated beings, cause is expressed by 'prior' and effect by 'subsequent.'" This is what the sages of the *Zohar and Midrash* indicate when referring to prior and subsequent. The first cause or first class of galaxies, known as the first universe, was established and emanated with the energy-intelligence of *Midat Ha'Din*, strict judgement of positive or negative activity. The Lord then brought the second stage of the universe into being. He added to the already existing energy-intelligences of negative and positive a third dimension energy-intelligence force of "compassion," known as the third column force of the universe. "There was no changing of the Lord's thought process. The second string of galaxies known as the second universe evolved through the natural law of cause and effect."[6]

Before exploring these subliminal concepts of creation, let us investigate the energy-intelligence systems that control the two cosmos. What is meant by *Midat Ha'Din* and *Midat Ha'Rahamin*? How do they differ from one another? The Lord, the cosmic designer, arranged the world for the purpose of removing the "Bread of Shame" concept.[7] Quite obviously, the universe had been programmed to evolve toward some final goal. The structured order of our universe toward an ultimate purpose is observed by the striking fact of the compliance of material entities with the natural laws and principles of our universe.

The argument for a grand design, a purpose to the universe, an orderly structure, points to the role of mankind in the universal scheme. Consciousness is a cosmic scenario. Yet, today man appears to play no role play within the cosmic mechanism, other than one of robotic consciousness. Mankind today, more than ever before, sees himself as nothing but another component of a massive computer, and for many, that computer is perceived as having surpassed the ability of a human being.

Thus, there was a grave and fundamental difficulty in reconciling the purpose of creation and the first incarnation of the universe, Cosmos I. *Midat Ha'Din* was strict judgment. Negative activity followed with an infusion of negative energy; positive activity brought with it the influence of positive energy. Strict judgment was firmly established and entrenched in the supernatural scheme of cosmological laws and principles. Man, it seemed, could not alter or redesign the cosmos.

Yet, the Bread of Shame dictum decreed that man surely could and would alter the influence of cosmic order. Was this possible? With Cosmos I in operation, the involuntary aspect of action and reaction were inevitable. The results were always the same. The Lord recognized the necessity for a cosmos permitting the existence of the mind as a separate entity that can act on matter causing it to behave in apparent violation of the natural laws and principles of the universe. Thus, a natural evolvement of Cosmos I into Cosmos II came into existence an interference to the otherwise normal operation of Cosmos I was planted in the universe that took over or at least impeded the operation of Cosmos I.

Suppose an individual were suddenly to commit an act of violence towards his fellow man. The natural laws and principles of Cosmos I dictate that the activities of this person have already determined the reaction, and thus there would follow a strict judgment of cause and effect, namely, the punishment for the crime of violence. Future events or reactions, being determined by our earlier decisions and actions, would dictate that future events would be entirely beyond our control. If, on the other hand, one chooses activities of a positive nature, strict judgement of Cosmos I dictates a determined positive reaction. Again, the natural laws and principles of Cosmos I assert the future events which lie outside the realm of personal control. Cosmos II added a third dimension: the energy-intelligence of restriction — the ability to nullify and temporarily force negative energy-intelligence to move in apparent violation of the laws of Cosmos I.

Cosmos I consisted of two fundamental energy-intelligences: *desire to share* and *desire to receive*, positive and negative, proton and electron. Following the original restriction due to Bread of Shame, one no longer could receive for oneself alone. If the decision to ignore this dictum was made, strict judgement was enforced. The punishment was hard and fast. In the universe of Cosmos I, we could control the causes of our decisions, but not the results or future events of those decisions.

Cosmos II changed allowed man to control his activities. He was offered the unique ability of influencing the structure of future events which had previously been strictly predetermined. The quality that allowed this new state of affairs to emerge was *Midat Ha'Rahamim*, the energy-intelligence of compassion.

Midat Ha'Rahmim changed time from absolute into a dimension of an elastic nature. Time is merely a frame of cause and effect. In Cosmos I, it was strict. Action was immediately followed by reaction. There was no opportunity or possibility for change. Cosmos II allowed time to expand and contract according to variable requirements. Time was no longer absolute. It became relative, subject to the intelligent energy of *Ra'hamim*, compassion. Thus was born the possibility of delayed reaction, a kind of animated suspension of predetermined events which provides time and enables the individual to go back in time, in a sense, and nullify previous decisions and actions.

This, in essence, is the realistic interpretation of *Teshuvah*, the word commonly translated as repentance. In fact this definition is a corruption of the cosmic code, because the literal translation of the Hebrew word *Teshuvah*[8] means "return." The word "repentance" ultimately made its way into the lexicon of all religions following this corruption. In any event, from a kabbalistic point of view, the *return* in time is a prerequisite for the nullification of negative activity.

Time is, in fact, a sequence of events, a definite number of connected phases branching from each other in the order of cause and effect.[9] Our sensation of time is somehow more a spiritual than a physical, bodily experience. We feel the passage of time differently. Two people working together in an office may experience the passage of an eight-hour day in a completely different way, one experiencing the quick passage of time, whereas for the other, the day may drag on interminably. The mutability of time is the mystery behind the energy-intelligence of *Midat Ha'Rahamim.*

Let us now explore another aspect of Cosmos II by raising the question as to why the kabbalists chose the Hebrew word *Ra'Hamim* (compassion) for their description of Cosmos II. Time traditionally has been regarded as a continuous, uniform regulator of activity. Yet, from a personal perspective, time is not uniform. Each of us sees and regards time with our own peculiar manipulating idea of reality. For this reason, the kabbalist created a figurative mode of speech, which referred to material objects, ideas and functions of every day life, employing the names of the tangible branches of the mundane world.

Each name explains its own metaphysical concept by pointing to the cosmic root which is located in the constellation of the celestial regions. If any idea of the cosmos were omitted, this would eventually result in a breach in the unity of the entire scope of cosmic comprehension and in the wisdom of the Kabbalah.[10] The language of the kabbalist dismantles the iron curtain surrounding modern astronomy and offers us the ability and the opportunity of perceiving the inner sanctum of the cosmos. Returning to the question as to why the kabbalist made use of the word *Ra'Hamim* to describe Cosmos II, let us closely examine this unique and often misunderstood term, "compassion." In a word, compassion means *Rega*, a Hebrew word translated as "one moment." But this is putting the cart before the horse. If anything, Cosmos II has become more confused than ever. How does this most often uttered word relate to the concept of compassion? In fact, when two Israelis engage in a heated exchange of thoughts, or a serious argument, the word "Rega" is pronounced as often as all other words combined.

One of the most interesting and in some way startling observations I have ever made was overhearing a one-sided conversation between two Israelis. The listener never said a word, but his voluble counterpart never ceased using the word "Rega," asking the listener to hear him out, as if his conversation was about to be interrupted. In fact, it never was, but the word "Rega" was constantly used, pleading for a moment to be heard. The moment to be heard continued for hours without interruption. So did the mention of the word *Rega*.

Unconsciously, the speaker was requesting patience of his listener that he might be heard without interruption. Only Israelis make use of the word *Rega* when there is no threat of not being heard by the listener. But, then again, Israelis display an impatience rarely found among others. They generally have no patience for listening themselves and so we might therefore assume, with a fairly high probability of accuracy, that subconsciously they expect their listener to abruptly terminate their train of thought — for that is what they would do if, so to speak, the conversational shoe were on the other foot! Hence, they find it necessary, through the constant use of the word *Rega*, to attempt to assure that others display the very *savlanut*, patience, for which they themselves have very little regard.

After much patient research into this matter, I have come to the conclusion that the Israeli has come under the cosmic control and influence of the Land of Israel.[11] This implies the cosmic characteristic both of the Land of Israel and the people of Israel, namely, *Am Segula*,[12] the three column system, directed and motivated by the energy-intelligence of the central column, referred to by the kabbalist as the intelligent energy of *Ra'Hamim*, or Cosmos II, which parallels the power of the neutron to maintain balance and stability between the proton and electron.

Just what is this mysterious internal metaphysical force of the neutron? *Rega*! Time! Compassion! The demand for patience! The energy-intelligence that requests time and patience rather than strict judgment. When negative activity becomes part of a cosmos, due to the negative thought processes and actions of man, the result and consequence of this activity assuredly is a reaction of negative energy-intelligence. This is Cosmos I.

Cosmos II, however, created a situation in which the immediate cosmic reaction would have to wait. Patience, Cosmos II, gives us a moment, a time of reprieve, the opportunity to set aside for a moment the laws and principles of strict judgement and display a little compassion. Time! Yet, the virtue of compassion is rarely observed.

When we have been hurt or wronged by our fellow man, the immediate reaction is one of strict judgment. How to settle the score or debt is immediate and uppermost in our minds. Seldom do we display the compassion that we ourselves, when on the other side of the fence, demand of others. We judge, in most cases, without stopping for a moment to reconsider all that has taken place. We refuse to permit the moment, Cosmos II, to be part of our cosmic order. We demand Cosmos II for ourselves when necessary, but for others, Cosmos I is fitting and appropriate. Compassion is something that we require, but to share compassion with others is another matter. We seek immediate justice and display no patience or injection of Cosmos II with its energy-intelligence of the power of *Rega*, the moment of compassion.

The energy-intelligences of Cosmos I or Cosmos II have no double standards. Invoking or drawing Cosmos I or Cosmos II depends entirely upon the activity of man. Man is the central and focal point of all cosmic activity. His display of compassion for his fellow man draws the cosmic order of Cosmos II into the universe whenever that display is made. His demand for strict judgement, rejecting outright the moment of patience, or compassion, infuses the cosmos with cosmic law of Cosmos I which holds no compassion either for others or for oneself. Consequently, when observing the chaotic condition of our universe, we have no one to blame but ourselves. We are witnessing the lack of *Rega*, time in human activity. Maybe the Israeli unconsciously recognizes this flaw in his activity and therefore continuously demands of others the *Rega*.

Whatever the case may be, Cosmos I and Cosmos II are integral parts of this grand universal scenario — and in that fact lies the dilemma of the scientist. Human activity, at present, is unstable. It see-saws back and forth from Cosmos I to Cosmos II. Due to the enlightenment of the Age of Aquarius,[13] with the advancements made by the science, we have begun to be conscious of internal, subatomic activity that seems to create uncertainty. Man, of all creation, is the least stable and his activity represents and displays this human instability. Hence, the findings of scientific research have become befuddled rather than enlightened. Yet, in a way it may be that we are becoming more enlightened because of scientific achievement, at least to the extent that in observing the metaphysical, subatomic realm of activity we shall now demand to know who or what is the cause of nature's instability and uncertainty.

The kabbalist asserts that humankind is behind it all, but that fortunately he has been provided with an antidote to cosmic upheaval: Rega! Time! Compassion! True, it may be a bit difficult to come by, but nevertheless it is possible to attain, and an enormous infusion of *Rega*, a time for compassion within the cosmos, will assure the dawning of the New Age.

This, then, was the concern of cosmic Yood. The assurance that human activity would overwhelmingly flood the Lord's battle station with *Rega*, Compassion, for this was the energy-intelligence that could overcome, once and for all, the threat of the Dark Lord and his Death Star fleet. No longer would there be need to fear the Empire of Impatience.

Was there a cosmic flaw inherent within creation? The scientific community claims that mass extinctions (most notably the one in which the dinosaurs perished) have repeatedly punctuated the history of life on this planet. These cataclysms seem to occur with striking precision and regularity, a fact which has given rise to a spectacular new theory that there may exist somewhere out in space a possible companion to the Sun, a Death Star for which has been coined the ominous cognomen, Nemesis. Galvanized by this radical proposal, astrophysicists have been searching the sky for an extraterrestrial intelligence capable of sending comets hurtling toward Earth.

From the kabbalistic point of view, the cosmos was created in perfect harmony. No cosmic flaw is allowed for in Genesis. The *Zohar*[14] assigns this role to the Milky Way — the celestial mechanism of which could explain the apparent clockwork regularity of the barrages from space. The extinction theories, however, seem to point to a world not exactly cast in the mold of the Garden of Eden. Even Noah's flood, according to the biblical account, could not be considered just cause for the disappearance of the dinosaurs from the earth. Yet, despite all of the information pointing to a history of catastrophic events and evidence of mass extinctions, we still have not the slightest clue as to what or who is behind it all.

"And the Lord said, 'Let there be a firmament in the midst of the waters.'[15] This is an allusion to the separation of the upper from the lower (immaterial from the material) through that negative aspect of existence which is known to kabbalists as the Left Column. Up until now, the first day, the text of Genesis has referenced only the positive Right Column, but here it alludes to the Left, indicating an increase of discord between the Left and the Right.[16] It is the nature of the Right to harmonize the whole, and therefore the whole is written with the Right since it is the source of harmony. But when the Left Column awoke, discord was awakened, and through that discord the wrathful fire was reinforced and there emerged from it the *Gehinnom* (Hell) which originated from the Left Column and continues there.

Moses, in his wisdom, pondered over this and drew a lesson from the work of creation. In the work of creation there was an antagonism of the Left against the Right, and the division between them allowed the Dark Lord to emerge and to fasten himself to the Left. Thankfully, the Central Column, the mediating principle, intervened on the third day and allayed the discord between the two sides, so that Gehinnom and the Dark Lord descended below. Thus the Left became absorbed in the Right and peace was restored."[17]

What seems to emerge from the *Zohar* is the

establishment of the Dark Lord and his Death Star fleet. However, to maintain harmony and stability within the Cosmos, the third day, or Central Column become an integral energy-intelligence force in the universe. The all embracing reality found expression as a unified whole.

"Hence we find twice written in the account of the third day, 'that it was good.'[18] This day became intermediary between two opposing sides and removed discord. It said to this side "good," and to the other side "good," and reconciled the two. Connected with this day is the secret of the name of the four letters (Tetragrammaton) engraved and inscribed."[19]

Thus, the state of the cosmos, its laws and principles with all the constituents of matter, all seem to have started without a flaw. The universe seemed to have emerged with a degree of order, coherent and organized. Our universe, from a kabbalistic view of the cosmos, was carefully fashioned and so is extraordinarily uniform. Our existence, along with that of the cosmos, did not result in and from a monstrous and meaningless cosmic accident. There is an apparent coherence of behavior over the whole cosmos. *Ra'Hamin* ruled supreme as the supernatural Force of the Lord's Empire, with antimatter as its energy-intelligence.

The cosmos, from a scientific world view, seemed to have developed a preference for matter (the energy-intelligence of the desire to receive for oneself alone). Chaos appears to dominate our terrestrial realm. The energy-intelligence of the Death Star appears to have overtaken the universe lock, stock, and barrel. All one has to do is to observe the perpetual conflict and confusion that goes on around us to see that the world is in disarray — this despite evidence to the contrary that there are fundamental constants in nature, certain quantities that play a role in physics and have the same *gematria*, or numerical value, anywhere and everywhere in the universe.

If there is cosmic design and order, then where is the evidence of it? Where is the antimatter that would prove nature's symmetry; where the *Myin Nukvin*, that King Solomon assured us exists in the universe? "The Lord created one against the other" declares the anonymous author of the beautiful esoteric rendering of Ecclesiastes.[20] The exploration of the subatomic world in the twentieth century has revealed the dynamic nature of energy and matter. Even at this level, one observes an interplay within the cosmic web in which particles are created and destroyed. Yet, how is it that, we and the things around us appear to be made up of only protons, electrons and neutrons without a trace of antimatter?

Another question Cosmic Yood raised for the purpose of understanding and coping with the chaotic conditions with which man ultimately would have to come to grips was, "Where is the invisible Death Star fleet located? Why can't we observe it? What is its activity? How can we detect its energy-intelligence?"

They hide behind the explosive flares, and within the collapsing and colliding stars, and with the rest of the cosmic chaos that rocks the celestial atmosphere. It is the insidious Death Star fleet that causes the magnetosphere to go into sudden and sporadic convulsions which dump millions of amperes of current into the polar region, giving rise to the aurora borealis.

"Observe that when the days of a man are firmly established in the supernal celestial, extraterrestrial grades, then man has a permanent place in the world. However, if man has not taken his rightful place in the cosmos of the outer space connection,[21] his days descend until they reach the cosmic level where the Dark Lord resides. The Angel of Death then receives authority to take away man's soul and pollute his body which remains permanently part of the dark side.

Happy are the righteous who have not polluted themselves and in whom no pollution has remained."[22]

The Death Star fleet, declares the *Zohar*, is based within the Milky Way. This is indeed a dramatic revelation. For most observers of the heavens, the Milky Way is an unexplored celestial continent filled with exotic beauty and serene entities of stellar dimensions. Yet, though she offers one of the most exciting, breathtaking views of an astronomer's paradise, beneath that fabric of space is woven the nemesis of mankind. The *Zohar* makes it quite clear how our existence, our character, is determined by the deep, interrelated connection between man and the cosmos.

"Come and see: In the center of the galaxy there is a celestial Dark Lord known as the Milky Way. All celestial entities, an endless and infinite array of them, revolve around it and are charged to keep watch over the secret deeds of human beings. In the same way, myriad emissaries go forth from the primeval celestial Dark Lord, the same Dark Lord by whom Adam was seduced. The Death Star fleet goes forth to spy out the secret deeds of mankind."[23]

In a cosmic perspective, most human concerns seem to be inextricably bound up in exquisite relationships with the heavens. Mass extinctions, as some scientists lead us to believe, are deeply rooted in the cosmos. Whether or not these devastating cosmic calamities took place precisely in the manner as set forth by scientists is not important. The question is why?

Most scientists favor extraterrestrial causes for mass extinctions, despite the lack of evidence of any event that would periodically disturb life on Earth or in outer space. The kabbalistic world view cites the Milky Way as the villain. "The star fleet of the Dark Lord is without a count, dependent on man's action," states the *Zohar*. The crowded Milky Way galaxy is a floating island comprised of over 100 billion stars, beautiful from afar, but also a terrifying force of potential disaster. The Death Star fleet is obviously capable of raining destruction from or upon its galaxy.

If this is so, then who is the Dark Lord that controls the Death Star fleet? Who commands the fleet to institute a reign of terror among the inhabitants of the galaxy? Who is this all-powerful being that rules over both celestial and terrestrial beings?

"R. Hiya discoursed on the verse: 'Thou has beset me behind and before and hast laid thine hand upon me.'[24] He said: "How greatly is it incumbent on the children of men to glorify the Lord! For when he created the world he looked on man and designed to make him to rule over all earthly things. He was of a dual form, righteous and dark, and resembled both celestial and earthly things. The Lord sent him down in Splendor, so that when the lesser creatures beheld the glory of his state, they fell down before him in awe, as it says: 'And the fear of you and the dread of you shall be upon every beast of the earth and upon every fowl of the earth.'[25]

R. Hiya continued: "The Lord brought him into the garden of His own planting, so that he might guard it and have endless joy and delight. Then the Lord gave him the commandment concerning the tree:[26] And alas! Man failed in his obedience. Had Adam been obedient he would have so dwelt forever, having eternal life and perpetual joy in the glory of the Garden."[27]

Had Adam never sinned, the Dark Lord and his Death Star fleet never could have raised their ugly heads. The galaxy and the earth would have been lovely places. The cosmos is all that is, was, or that ever will be. The fall of Adam changed everything. His deviation from the path of virtue left the entire cosmos in a state of distress and diminution. The spiritual, celestial realm along with the terrestrial, physical universe suffered from this same debasement.

The face of the galaxies, the appearance of earth and the universe beyond, all changed from a scene of serenity and quiescence to one of chaos and catastrophe. The universe became anything but a Garden of Eden. Scientists have sufficient evidence that the universe is materially asymmetrical.

"According to tradition, the fleshy part of Adam's heel outshone the orb of the sun. Said R. Elazar: After Adam sinned, his beauty was diminished and his height was reduced to a hundred cubits. However, before the Fall, Adam's height reached to the first firmament."[28] Have there been mass extinctions in the past? According to the *Zohar*, dinosaurs and other primeval life did not become extinct. They still exist now as they did before. If this is the case, then are these former plant and animal species that apparently inhabited our planet and where is the agent that initiates the apparent clockwork regularity of celestial bombardments?

The *Zohar* strongly implicates man as the mechanism behind all cosmic activity. The Death Star fleet of the Milky Way rains death and destruction when human activity embraces negative behavior. The energy-intelligence of negative human behavior consists principally of a submission to "the desire to receive for oneself alone," as, similarly, did the sin of Adam.[29] The infusion of cosmic negative energy into the cosmos fuels the Death Star fleet in their function of materially making manifest the energy-intelligence of human cosmic negativity.

Life in the galaxies has and will continue to be controlled by astronomical events, but only to the extent and limit of the intelligent energy of human activity. Yet, for all the evidence of destruction, the universe after the Fall of Adam, from time to time, experienced the serenity of the Garden of Eden. "It is written: 'King Solomon made him a *palanquin* (*apiryon*) of the trees of Lebanon.'[30] "*Apiryon*" symbolizes the Palace below which is formed in the likeness of the Palace above. This the Lord called the Garden of Eden.[31]

During the Temple period, states the *Zohar*,[32] the universe returned to its former cosmic position. Earth itself experienced an era of peace and a degree of tranquillity surpassed only by that which Adam knew in the Garden of Eden. Human activity was impressed with *Myin Nukvin*, the anti-matter of Eden. We can therefore ascertain that the cosmos, while undergoing apparent change by and within itself, maintains a parallel original universe. The alteration of the cosmos, as we mortals perceive it, happens solely on a physical, material level. Intrinsically, on the metaphysical level, nothing changes. Substitution takes place exclusively in a corporeal realm.

As Adam went, so goes the universe. When Adam's corporeal framework declined in size, so did all other species of plant and animal life. The physical universe, with all its infinite galaxies, underwent the same kind of contraction. The dinosaur shrunk to the size of a lizard and the pterodactyl became a bird! Plants and insects became like little cousins of their very much larger brothers and sisters. The real universe, however, the metaphysical universe did not undergo any form of extinction or mutation.

Materially, the cosmos is asymmetrical; internally, it is symmetrical in every way. The metaphysical universe is the absolute picture of perfection: predictable, highly ordered — it is the Garden of Eden, which soon will return to its original pristine splendor. The Age of Aquarius has brought the turnaround to an expanding universe, both spiritually and cosmically. Paradoxically, the New Age is also responsible for the success of high technology in man's search for infinite reductions of material processes, such as fiber optics and the splitting of atoms. At the same time, wherever we set our eyes, from the far-flung galaxies to the innermost recesses of the atom, we discover uniformity and an elaborate organizational structure.

It should follow, therefore, that our universe conforms to the beauty and elegance of atomic harmony. However, everywhere we look we see evidence of an irregular, chaotic universe — manifested cosmically by celestial bombardment, and on the earthly level by man's inhumanity to his fellow man. How can these two seemingly opposing forces, order and chaos, possibly be harmonized?

The cosmos, connected with the celestial Age of Aquarius reveals the wonder of nature's intrinsic beauty and order. Spiritual man frequently experiences the cosmic connection with the all embracing unified reality. Materialistic, self-centered, ego-minded individuals, are the true culprits. They refuse to let go of the illusion that gives preference to cosmic disunity. *Myin Nukvin*, compassion, is not in their spiritual lexicon. And so they go on, little knowing that it is their negative activity that fuels the machinery of the Dark Lord and his Death Star fleet. We humans are responsible for the chaotic universe — just as the blame may be laid on Adam for the transformation of dinosaurs into lizards!

How is it that the physical universe remains spatially symmetrical? Were it not symmetrical, the planets' orbits around the sun would keep changing as the solar system rotates around the Milky Way.

"And the righteous are the world's foundation," declares the author of Proverbs.[33] Earth and the galaxies, are conspicuously made of ordinary matter. Yet, as previously mentioned, from the zoharic point of view, it is *Myin Nukvin*, the anti-matter energy-force that maintains stability within the cosmos.

"R. Isaac once asked R. Shimon to explain how it is that some say the world is founded on seven pillars and some on one pillar, to wit, the *Zaddik*, the Righteous. R. Shimon replied: "It is all the same. There are seven, but among these is one called *Zaddik* on which the rest are supported. Hence it is written: 'The Righteous One (*Zaddik*) is the foundation of the world.'"[34]

Throughout history, it has been taken for granted that intelligent energy was, in the main, a positive quality. The kabbalist knew that the cosmos originated with positive and negative energy, the former a cause and the latter its effect.[35] This diametrically opposed union of opposites was the Cosmos I effect. However, when Cosmos II came into existence, meaning that the mediating principle or Central Column became established, humankind no longer remained merely a participator within the cosmos. He became a determinator. It therefore became necessary for the existence of the universe in each generation to have a permanent team of *Zaddikim* (Righteous Ones) to prevent the annihilation of the cosmos by the Dark Lord. These Righteous Ones maintained a sufficient reserve of *Myin Nukvin* to assure a spatially symmetrical universe.

The rest was left to man, either to fulfill the purpose of creation and thereby vaporize the Death Star fleet, or to succumb to the energy-intelligence of "the desire to receive for oneself alone" and permit the rulership of the Dark Lord's empire over the entire cosmos. The difficulty in overcoming the Death Star fleet was obvious. The problem that seemed to rule out the other letters in the creation scenario remained. Humankind needed a special cosmic support that would provide Earth's inhabitants with a fighting chance.

Cosmic Yood believed that she had the specific energy-intelligence capable of waging a successful battle with the Dark Lord's empire. The Tetragrammaton,[36] the four-lettered code name of the Lord, was her secret weapon. By means of this cosmic channel, Moses slew the Egyptian.[37] The Tetragrammaton contained the highest undiluted and untransformed state of energy imaginable.

R. Shimon continued: "We have a tradition that when the Lord created the world, He engraved into the midst of the mysterious, ineffable and most glorious lights, the letters *Yood*, *He*, *Vav*, and *He*. They are in themselves the synthesis of all worlds both above and below. The upper was brought to completion by the cosmic influence of the energy-intelligence of the letter Yood embodying the primordial celestial point which issued from the perfectly concealed and unknowable, the mysterious Infinite, En Sof.

Out of the imperceptible Endless issued a slender thread of light which was itself concealed and invisible, but which yet contained all other lights. The light which came forth from the slender light is mighty and frightful."[38]

The *Zohar* adds a strong holistic flavor to the quantum aspects of the nature of energy with the assertion that everything is made up of everything else. Yet there remained a display of a hierarchy within the cosmic structure. It is within the all embracing unity of the Yood that the constituents of energy and matter became the ultimate, unified force.

As such, Yood contended that her dimension of light, combined with her energy-intelligence of the grand unification in the creative process of the world, assuredly would bring about the final correction to the world. The response of the Lord to Yood's plea was fast in coming. The energy emitted by the plea, as stated before, established the energy-intelligence of *Myin Nukvin*. Here was the opportunity the Dark Lord had been waiting for, but never thought would become a reality, the possibility of making contact with Yood's intelligent energy.

The command of the Lord was loud and clear. "*Dy Loh*! Stop right where you are!"[39] By extending beyond the protection of the cosmic shield, Yood provided the Death Star with the needed advantage of ruling over galactic space, the world of good and evil, the universe of corruption. Mere contact with the Death Star would prevent cosmic Yood from regaining her place in the Tetragrammaton. The world of Action, Earth's cosmic universe is governed by change — from correction before the sin of Adam, to corruption and once again back to emendation. For this reason, the Tetragrammaton is pronounced "Adonoy"[40] and not its original pronunciation.

Thus, the Yood was told to keep her place. Were she to be used in the creation of the World, she would then stand the chance of becoming corrupted. This would have the effect of rooting out the Yood from the Holy Name. In the Holy Name no corruption ever takes place. This cosmic process is revealed in the words of the Prophet, "For I the Lord change not."[41]

Cosmic Yood dares not descend to support the World of Action, for she might become entrapped and corrupted by the Dark Lord. When the universe, by positive human activity, is elevated to the outer space connection and thus completion, the Tetragrammaton will then be pronounced as written. This cosmic phenomena will only come to be recognized upon completion of the process of *Tikune* (Correction).[42]

Changes, dynamic interplays of the cosmos, unusual supernovae, dinosaurs turning into lizards, these are phenomena that exist in the unreal cosmic dimension of the World of Action, a universe in which Earth and man are very much integral parts. Defects, celestial barrages, and corruption are aspects of this world's normal existence inasmuch as man himself is fragmented.

Technological advances help us to uncover many "new" cosmic features, yet the discovery of each new phenomenon relates to the cosmos of change, the unreal rather than the all embracing unified reality. This was no place for cosmic Yood. Thus, the Lord said to her: "You are engraven within me, marked within me and My desire and energy intelligence is in you. Consequently, you are not the suitable cosmic channel for creation."[43]

17

The Letters Tet and Het

Ben Azzai said: The reward of a good deed is another good deed, and the reward of transgression is another transgression.

(Ethics of the Fathers, Ch.IV)

THE FACE OF THE EARTH, THE FACE OF OUR ENTIRE planetary system, the view of our galaxy, and of the infinite universe beyond, all would undergo the numerous changes that human activity assigned to them. They were all aspects of the physical uncertainty that belonged to the realm of changing illusions. With planets on their permanent orbits, with satellites rotating with clockwork precision, and seasons coming uninterrupted in their order, man had little reason to believe he had any hand in the cosmic scenario of colliding galaxies, celestial barrages, and comet attacks. For most of human existence, the Lord provided the necessary protection against almost every cosmic cause for alarm. Rays from the cosmos are kept well in hand by a magnetic shield. Destructive radiation is restrained by the ionosphere. The earth seems assured of the right measure of heat and the correct atmosphere for the life processes.

Despite the truly dangerous games that man has been playing by splitting atoms and genes, the real threat to humankind's existence is the Death Star fleet, which continues unabated in its pursuit of dominion over the universe. Pitted against the Dark Lord, man has not fared well. Inhumanity reigns supreme. With this perspective of a future cosmos, Cosmic Tet approached the Lord to enter her plea as the suitable celestial channel for the crowning creation of the world. Cosmic Yood, for all her positive energy-intelligence-force, was needed at *G'mar Ha'Tikune*, the final correction period. Her position within the Tetragrammaton could, under no circumstances, be placed in jeopardy.

"O Lord of the universe, may it please Thee to create the world with me, since through me Thou art called "Tov" (Good) and "Yashar" (Righteous). The initial letter of the word "Tov" begins with the letter "Tet," indicative of my internal energy-intelligence which is good, proper and positive."[1]

Tet's particular energy-intelligence was precisely the panacea needed to alleviate every danger and onslaught originating from the Death Star. In such an optimal environment, humankind very well might achieve its objective, the removal of negative energy. Provided and fueled with sufficient streams of positive energy, man would be prepared to begin the great battle to restore harmony in the cosmos. A return to the cosmic order of the Garden of Eden, the pre-Fall of Adam's days, seemed certain with Cosmic Tet as the architect of a new era.

"'And the Lord saw the light that it was good.'[2] Every dream that contains the term *Tov* presages peace above and below, provided the letters are seen in their proper order. These letters, Tet, Vav, and Beth, afterwards were combined to signify the Righteous One (*Zaddik*) of the world. As it is written,[3] 'Say of the righteous one that he is good,' because the supernal radiance is contained therein."

In the foregoing chapters, we have searched across the range of kabbalistic teachings and discovered some radical new ideas about creation, astral influences, space and time, order and chaos, a meaningful universe, and an understanding of man and his cosmic environment. Much of what has been presented will undoubtedly raise some eyebrows and draw its share of criticism. It would be foolish to deny that many of the readers of this book will reject outright some of the ideas presented by the kabbalists. However, this is par for the course when any new approach to an understanding of creation, the universe, and man's role and relationship in it, is advanced. Nevertheless, the kabbalistic view of the universe illustrates the kind of ideas that cannot be ignored, especially in light of some of the recent advances in quantum physics and their inherent uncertainty.

Quantum Theory permits the possibility that events which happen in the subatomic or in the metaphysical world occur without causes. Particles seem to appear out of nowhere with no apparent causation. Most religious philosophies incorporate the kabbalistic doctrine of Bread of Shame.[5] To get something out, you must put something in — this is the basic formula we learn as children. Yet the new physics presents a new scenario that incorporates the essence of the cosmic flow found within the concept of Bread of Shame.

Discussing this scenario, the physicist Alan Guth remarked, "It is often said that there is no such thing as a free lunch. The universe, however, is a free lunch."[6]

I personally consider the appearance of a particular aspect of quantum mechanics to be a direct validation of the kabbalistic understanding of the question of existence, in that quantum theory breaks a deadlock that has existed between religion and science that has been in place for several hundred years. The laws of Newtonian physics are simply invalid in the subatomic realm — which proves, once and for all, the kabbalistic belief that religion is a myth, but then again, so is science.

However, the possibility, advanced by quantum theory, that space-time could arise out of nothingness, as a result of a causeless conversion, seems to contradict everything around us. Using the kabbalistic dictum that there is sense to what makes sense, a different, more realistic, perspective may be achieved relative to quantum mechanics, which will perhaps prove to be more valid than that of the scientists themselves. When some entity apparently appears where none existed before, do not assume it is without specific causation. Drown your ego. Leave ignorance on the doorstep where it belongs. An overly rational approach to such questions reflects only our inability to *consciously* grasp the activity of cause and effect — when, in fact, our everyday consciousness, the five senses alone, are wholly incapable of perceiving the metaphysical basis of reality.[7] From a kabbalistic point of view, the origin of the universe, the laws of nature, all revolve around and evolve from a basic cause: the removal of Bread of Shame.

The Age of Aquarius is indeed the Age of Enlightenment. Quantum theory confronts both religion and science with the same questions that Kabbalah has been addressing for centuries: Is there good and evil? If there is a Creator, why does he remain beyond our finite perceptions? What are the underlying causes of existence? Can we be responsible for our acts in a world where events occur without cause?

As does the new physics, Kabbalah addresses itself to the central issues of causality, questions of morality, right or wrong, good and evil. No longer can those who formerly worshiped solely at the alter of the great gods, Science and Technology, avoid these questions and dispel them as meaningless. Thus we find that as scientific understanding of our cosmos advances, science inadvertently provides the very conceptual framework necessary in improving our understanding of Kabbalah and the cosmic code contained within the Bible.

Since the advent of Newtonian classical physics, there has existed a dichotomy between religion and science. For the kabbalist, no conflict ever existed between religion and science. Religion is a myth. Only the Creator is real. The Bible is not a religious document of doctrine. Buried beneath the Torah's literal interpretation is the answer to the secret of life's origin, the true nature of which it is the purpose of Kabbalah to decipher. Central to the truth, as perceived by the ancient kabbalists, is the idea of a beautiful cosmos of harmony, symmetry, and with man in the role as its determinator. The entire physical universe is the medium of expression of the desire of man.

What does it really mean when the Bible states that the Lord caused the creation to come into existence? How is creation affected by the role of man as determinator? The word creation carries with it a variety of meanings. The creation of the universe, from a kabbalistic point of view, is taken to mean the creation of energy-intelligences to provide the intelligent energy of free will, as exemplified by the *desire to receive*, with the opportunity of removing Bread of Shame.[8] The creation of the observable physical world, including space and time, permitted man the corporeal expression of the *desire to receive*, to achieve this objective.

The Creator's withdrawal and restriction (Tsimtsum) were, consequently, a necessary prerequisite of creation. He was then and remains now the true Composer of all creation. However, as no negativity (*desire to receive*) could exist in his endlessly positive presence, the Creator restricted Himself to allow his creations, the souls of man, the opportunity of removing Bread of Shame. The Lord orchestrated celestial and terrestrial activity based on human activity. Simply stated, He shifted his activity from one as composer to arranger. Henceforth, after the creation, the music of the universe would depend upon the behavior of man.

The biblical code contains the natural laws and principles for an orderly universe. The essential feature in all of these laws is the subsequent removal of Bread of Shame. By man's involvement he can open the gates of his own being, revealing a universe of endless beauty and perfect harmony. The old idea of man's purpose in the universe, in which his only function is to "serve the Lord," was thus swept away by the factor of self determination.

Consequently, armed with this information, the path is

clear for a simplified explanation of the difference between good and evil. Goodness stems from those activities that take into account the purpose of creation, and its underlying thought process, namely the removal of Bread of Shame, while that which is evil does not.

However, not all negative energy-intelligences are necessarily evil. The *desire to receive for the sake of sharing*, while intrinsically negative, nevertheless conforms to the natural laws of the universe. The negative inclination is a necessary factor in the continued existence of the world,[9] for without it no one would build a house, marry, raise a family, or engage in trade.[10] Nevertheless, it is within man's grasp to control negative energy-intelligences, against whose power the cosmic code of the Bible is an antidote.[11] This control permitted man to make manifest a physically expressed universe in harmony with the all embracing unified reality of the Lord.

Perhaps the most widely accepted explanation of suffering in the world is that the righteous undergo punishment for every small sin they have committed. Then they can enjoy their full reward in the world to come. The question of the origin and meaning of "world to come" posed a number of theological questions, which the Sages have attempted to solve in a variety of ways. First, there is the issue of where this "world" may be. Another vexing problem is why we must wait until after death to merit the entrance in the "world to come?"

This problem is dealt with in a number of different ways. On the one hand, is the view that the issue is beyond the grasp of man's intellect, in support of which the verse, "The secret things belong unto the Lord" may be quoted.[12] On the other hand, a series of partial solutions is offered. From a kabbalistic point of view, the world to come exists presently for those who can connect with it — a place where cosmic consciousness begins, and where the limitations of time, space, and motion have no dominion.

Viewing the cosmos as it emerged, the Lord said, "It is good."[13] Before the sin of Adam, negative energy-intelligence did not exist as there was no violation of the doctrine of Bread of Shame. Human activity that stays clear of the "free lunch" concept, grants assurance that one is a *Ben Olam Habah*, a son of the world to come. When man adheres to the laws and principles of the world of reality, he does not submit to a free lunch. The individual for whom the concept of Bread of Shame means nothing is hitching a ride to nowhere on transportation provided by the physical world of illusion.

"The Zaddik will be rewarded with material prosperity, and his merit will endure forever."[14] The *Zohar*[15] describes the righteous as individuals whose behavior brought a cosmic connection to the energy-intelligence of *Ze'ir Anpin*, or the *Sfirotic* consciousness of Yesod (Foundation). This realm — a state of cosmic presence — is no different from conditions encountered by a spacecraft escaping the Earth's gravitational attraction. Upon entering space, it is governed by the application of a new set of laws and principles regarding time, space and motion.[16]

"'And it came to pass after these things that his master's wife....'[17] R. Hiya discussed the text: 'Bless the Lord, you angels of his, you who are mighty in strength, that fulfill his word, hearkening unto the voice of his word.'[18] R. Hiya interpreted this to mean: How greatly it behooves a man to guard against sin and to pursue the straight path, so that the Dark Lord, his daily assailant, should not lead him astray. And since he assails man perpetually, it behooves man to muster all his force against him and to entrench himself in the place of strength; for as the Dark Lord is mighty, it behooves man to be mightier still. Such a one was Joseph, who was called righteous and guarded in purity the sign of the holy covenant which was imprinted upon him. (Joseph refused to submit to temptation of the free lunch).

R. Eleazar said: The word, after,[19] "ahar" here alludes to the Dark Lord, being the name of the other side. Joseph exposed himself to his onslaught by paying enormous attention to his personal appearance. That gave an opening to the Dark Lord to say: 'Behold! Joseph's father Jacob observes mourning for him (Joseph) and he decks himself out and curls his hair!'(Joseph did not, at that moment, feel compassion for his father's anguish over his disappearance and assumed death). "Thus, the bear was let loose, as it were, and set upon him."[20]

The biblical account of Joseph and his brothers has, for most readers of the Bible, been another beautiful and tragic story of family strife and difficulty. The *Zohar* perceives the narration as part of the overall cosmic code revealed in the Bible. Astronomy, astrology, social behavior, and cosmic connections are but some of the revealing features surrounding the Jacob and Joseph story. Of all the Genesis narratives, those about Joseph are the longest and most detailed. They are not a collection of isolated and fragmentary incidents. The account contains an unprecedented wealth of background material in cracking the cosmic code. From this point of view, it provides the greater opportunity in our quest for the grand unification theory.

The Central Column, the cosmic glue for the grand unification theory, is clearly demonstrated within the Joseph narration. The focus of attention in the Genesis narrative is the nobility of Joseph's character and the salvation that came through his compassion. The *Midrash* also softens the harsh treatment accorded by Joseph to his brothers, and points out that, "he had behaved like a brother to them when they were in his power, while they had not treated him like a brother when he was in their power."[21] His brother, Shimon, who had cast Joseph into the pit,[22] was ostensibly chained by Joseph, but as soon as the other brothers had left, "he gave him to eat and drink, and bathed and anointed him."[23]

Joseph was present at his father's death. At this point, the brothers apparently feared that Joseph would take revenge for their cruel treatment of him in his youth.[24] He, however, dispelled their fears by citing once again his cosmic energy-intelligence, Yesod (foundation), and demonstrating compassion. Joseph had every reason to disregard this attribute because his brothers were completely alienated from him.

Joseph symbolized the epitome of the grand unification energy-intelligence, *Rehamim*, known as the cosmic *sfirotic* effect of "foundation." The name implied its function within the cosmos. The biblical noun *rahamim* and the verb *raham* or *riham*, frequently used to denote this behavior, are derived from the same root as the noun *rehem*, (womb). Some scholars of the Bible have proposed that its original meaning was "brotherhood," as those born from the same womb usually express a brotherly attitude towards each other. For King David, the concept indicated an essential relationship between the Lord, the Force, and those the Bible refers to as the Israelites. Those souls originating from the positive energy-intelligence of Abel are known as Israelites, a term noted to indicate the fundamental characteristic of *Tov*, good. The other peoples of the Earth whose souls are rooted in the negative intelligence of Abel are *Erev Rav*, the nation of mixed multitudes. They are understood through the description of certain forms of conduct as displayed by unloving and misanthropic individuals.[25]

"He, the Lord, being full of compassion, forgives iniquity and does not destroy," declares King David.[26] "Learn to do well, seek justice, relieve the oppressed, judge the fatherless, plead for the widow," pleads the prophet Isaiah.[27] These verses were understood to sum up and explain the grand unification energy-intelligence of the Lord, the attribute of compassion. They were meant to establish the norm for human conduct.

"Just as the Lord is referred to as compassionate and gracious, so must you be compassionate and gracious, giving gifts freely."[28] Therefore, thou shall keep the commandments of the Lord, to walk in his ways and to fear him."[29]

The Talmud expanded and deepened the Biblical concept by recognizing the energy-force of compassion as a vital characteristic of the Israelite, as opposed to the *Erev Rev*.[30] Maimonides declared that arrogant, cruel and unloving people were to be suspected of not being Israelites.[31] In this connection, attention must be directed above all to the new meaning infused into the idea of Jew and non-Jew by R. Isaac Luria and his Lurianic system of Kabbalah. This restatement of an ancient conception actually represents one of the most important constituent elements of Kabbalism. In all the numerous references to this subject in the Talmud and the Midrashim, there is none as startling and revealing as the Lurianic interpretation of this most delicate issue.

After the exodus from Spain, Jewish thought in general and the Kabbalah in particular underwent a complete transformation, a catastrophe of such overwhelming proportions that it uprooted the Golden Age of the Jewish people and affected every sphere of Jewish thought and understanding. It was in the great upheaval of that crucial period, that Kabbalah established its claim to spiritual domination within Judaism.

The writings of the ancient Spanish kabbalists, dating from Talmudic and post-Talmudic days, were essentially the privilege of a small group of mystics. The kabbalists of the time were a small group of esoterics who were not intent on spreading the Kabbalah. After the catastrophe of the Spanish expulsion, there arose deep-seated feelings as to the religious significance and the innermost content of their expulsion. This expression was achieved in the far-reaching changes in the outlook on life in general and their surroundings in particular. Considerable numbers of Spanish Jews, including the chief Rabbi Abraham Seneor and most of the members of the influential families, preferred baptism to exile.

In the wake of this spiritual and material upheaval, many exiled Jews settled in the ancient city of Safed. A group of Jewish mystics were setting the stage in new religious conceptions to which the Kabbalah of Safed laid claim. They shaped new attitudes and customs as their "Golden Age" was ripped away. They began to seek an understanding of their suffering in one of the darkest annals of Jewish history.

During this period, the Jewish people were separated from other peoples as a result of their acceptance of monotheism. The acknowledgment of a single Creator was the distinguishing characteristic of the Jewish people, for they had completely discarded idolatry — the practice of which was uniformly characteristic of the non-Jew. Both the *Zohar*[32] and the *Talmud*[33] describe this division in terms of, Jew and *okum*, the latter being an abbreviated term for *oved kohavim u-mazzalot*, a worshipper of stars and planets.

The biblical conception of, and the attitude toward, the non-Jew by the Jew are strikingly different today than those expressed during the Talmudic period. Biblical Israel was acquainted with two classes of *gerim* (strangers), resident aliens, usually proselytes and foreigners who considered their residency in the land more or less temporary.[34] The latter were referred to as *zarim* or *nokhrim*, terms generally applied to anyone outside the framework of the Jewish nation.

"And the Lord said to Moses and Aaron, this is the ordinance of the Passover (lamb): There shall no *nekhor* (strangers) eat thereof."[35] This biblical prohibition forbade the stranger from participating in the observance of the Passover lamb. However, the terms, *nekhor* and *gerim* also applied to a Jew. The word "*ger*," for instance, in late Second Temple times, became virtually synonymous with the proselyte, a converted non-Jew who was admitted to the religious fellowship of Israel.

As stated, the word *ger* in the Bible is taken to refer to the proselyte. The *ger toshav*,[36] the "resident stranger," was regarded as belonging to a different and particular character. He was a non-Jew who accepted some, but not all, of the commandments of the Torah. As a result, he was permitted to reside in the energy-charged land of Israel and enjoy many of the privileges enjoyed by the Israelites.

This is not a book about *halakha*, accepted decisions in rabbinic law or those parts of the Talmud concerned with legal matters. In particular, I make no attempt to discuss religious law or questions of who is or is not a Jew or non-Jew. Nor is it a book of religion. Rather, it is about the impact of the penetrating kabbalistic world view of the Force of the Lord, as it makes its way towards physical expression. It is a book about power, the majestic power of the Lord.

This work is primarily intended for the general reader with no previous knowledge of religion. The central theme of the book concerns what I call the forces of the Lord and the Death Star fleet of the Dark Lord. It may seem bizarre, but in my opinion, what were formerly questions bound up with religious dogma now can seriously be understood from a universal scientific point of view. Occasionally, it becomes necessary to explain some *halakha* in careful detail, but I do not make any claim that my observations must necessarily be complete. The correctness of the details is not important. What matters is that the kabbalistic world view of our universe provides the possibility of penetrating the meaning of our cosmos and of ourselves.

The impact of religion on society has been a mixed blessing. There is no denying that many cases of selfless devotion by the religious community have been recorded throughout history, however, many religionists long ago became institutionalized, and began to concern themselves more with power and politics than with good and evil. In our own time, religious hatred and hostility fester all over the world. While most religions extol the virtues of "love thy neighbor," it is all too often hatred, arrogance, and war that characterize the history of the world's great religious institutions.

Few would deny that religion has set a divisive example

in society, rather than trying to be a positive force, pulling all peoples toward completion of the world's rectifications. The sad history of bigotry seemed inevitable once religious organizations became institutionalized. As a result, today we see tremendous dissatisfaction with religious establishments in the Western world. Many have turned elsewhere in their search for spiritual enlightenment and fulfillment.

Kabbalah, through the effort and writings of R. Ashlag, reveals more of the deeper meaning of existence, good and evil, than can be found in many, if not all, traditional religions. Through his efforts we now understand the magnitude of the iniquity committed by those nations and religions which embitter minorities and strip them of their freedom, dignity, and ancient customs. Historically, the downfall of nations came about solely as a result of the oppression of minorities and individuals who eventually overcame and destroyed their oppressors. It is now clear to everyone that worldly peace cannot be established if we do not consider the freedom of the individual. Without it, there can be no lasting peace.

Thus far, we have defined the individual as in terms of how society nurtures him. Yet, a question remains — where is the individual himself? Surely an individual is more than that which he inherits from his ancestors. Where is the individual, the inheritor? Where is the separate entity we can define as the "self?" The self is central to all creation. It does not depend upon which religion, culture, or politics. The egotistic opposition between people, the ever-sharpening international tensions, will not disappear through any political, cultural, or religious stratagem, whatever it may be.

The prophet Isaiah, in his prophecy of peace said, "And

the wolf shall dwell with the lamb, and the leopard shall lie down with the kid."[37] The reason he gives for this is, "for the earth shall be full of knowledge of the Lord, as the waters cover the sea."[38] The prophet attributes worldly peace to full of knowledge of the Lord.[39]

There is the key: Knowledge of the Force of the Lord and the Dark Side. "All mankind will be united into a single body with a single mind, filled with the knowledge of the Lord,"[40] declares R. Ashlag. Let us now turn to R. Isaac Luria's new interpretation of the idea of the Israelite and the other nations. Moses said to the Lord: "And if thou deal thus with me, kill me, I pray thee, out of hand, if I have found favor in thy eyes, let me not see my wickedness."[41]

Exploring this unusual plea by Moses, the Ari, R. Luria, raises the question as to why the verse seems to refer to the wickedness of Moses when in fact it was the people who seem to be at fault. The verse, in his view, should have stated "their wickedness" and not "my wickedness."

The souls of Moses originated from Abel. The souls of Balaam stemmed from Abel as well. Consequently, they both issued from the same source. But when the serpent infused Eve with venom, the intelligence of evil, from that point on, all offspring and subsequent descendants were co-mingled with both good and evil. Moses grew out of the energy-intelligence of goodness, whereas Balaam, the wicked, issued from the intelligent energy of evil.

The Zohar states that the leaders of the *Erev Rav*, the mixed multitudes, were the children of Balaam, Yunus, and Yumbrus.[42] For this reason Moses concerned himself with converting the mixed multitudes from their evil inclination which originated and stemmed from Abel. Moses and the *Erev Rav* were *interrelated*. The *Erev Rav* were responsible for the making of the Golden Calf.[43] They were the evil manifestation of Israel which exists to this very day. The *Erev Rav* emerged from the same source as Moses.[44]

This, then, was the implication of the Lord's advice to Moses, "Go thee down for the people (and not the Lord's people) which thou broughtest out of the land of Egypt have corrupted themselves."[45] Moses, consequently, pleaded on behalf of the nation of Israel — the segment of Israel, the *Erev Rav*, the evil aspect of Abel, his (Moses') other half. "Wherefore should the Egyptians speak, and say, for mischief did He bring them out, to slay them in the mountains, and to consume them from the face of the Earth. Turn from Thy wrath and display compassion of this evil by the people."[46] They were the people of Moses. He brought them into the nation of Israel and he pleaded on their behalf for the purpose of cleansing and elevating this evil energy-intelligence so as to make it do only good.

Throughout the Bible we read of a nation never ceasing to be dissatisfied, ever complaining and never recalling the good the Lord had provided for them. When again, as many times before, "the mixed multitude that was among them felt a lust, they wept again, and said Who shall give us flesh to eat? But now our soul is dried away."[47] And Moses said unto the Lord: "Why hast thou afflicted thy servant? I am not able to bear all this people alone, because it is too heavy for me. And if Thou deal thus with me, kill me, I pray Thee, out of hand, if I have found favor in Thy eyes, let me not see (the portion of evil that is co-mingled within me) my wickedness."

"With this understanding," continues R. Luria, "an insight

will be gained of the coded verse, 'and there never arose a prophet since, in Israel, like Moses, whom the Lord knew face to face,'[48] and its Midrashic interpretation that, 'within Israel shall never arise one as Moses, but amongst the other nations of the world, there shall appear a prophet as Moses.'"[49] Both Balaam and Moses issued from the same source. We can additionally understand the saying of the Sages, "The blessings upon the nation of Israel ought to have been accorded by way of Moses." They were presented by the leading authority of black magic, Balaam himself,[50] the purpose being to transmute the energy-intelligence of evil, as portrayed by the evil aspect of Israel, Balaam, and thus, undergo a transformation from evil to good.

The two Hebrew letters, Beth and Lamed, forming the name of Balaam were, by design, the same two letters included within the Abel's name. The "Hay" of Moses' name was included within the first letter "Hay" of Abel's name. For this very reason did the Bible indicate the essence of Moses and his origination from the energy-intelligence of good by stating in coded form, "And the woman conceived, and bore a son, (Moses). And when she saw him that he was a *goodly* child, she hid him three months."[51] For Moses stemmed from the positive, good aspect of Abel.[52]

This is a most revealing interpretation concerning the nation of Israel: They consisted of good and evil. This intense evil later became incorporated within the nation of Israel by Moses. The express purpose for Moses' action was to facilitate the *G'mar Ha'Tikune*, the Final correction. For this reason, the original "Noahide Laws"[53] were insufficient in achieving the Final Correction. The energy-intelligence of evil, implanted in Eve by the serpent, was far too strong to be overcome by the seven restrictive channels of the Noahide Laws. The task was formidable. Nothing short of the revelation on Mount Sinai, the Torah and commandments, could assure the mastery of the Lord over the Death Star fleet, the dominion of good over the energy-intelligence of evil.

This is the meaning of the statement by the Sages that, "the commandments were given for the purpose of bringing human beings together."[54] We now can understand the words of Hillel, the prince, to the convert. He told him that the central axis of the Torah is, "Love thy neighbor as thyself."[55] The rest of the 612 commandments between man and the Lord are in the category of preparation for this single precept, Love thy neighbor. R. Akiba declared, "this is an important principle in the Torah."[56]

The intelligent energy of good becomes physically expressed when man's actions are performed in a manner to impart to others. Humankind thus is principally divided into two basic categories, the "Israelite" and *Erev Rav*." We are not concerned in this book with the descendants of Cain. This matter will be discussed in *Wheels of a Soul II*.

The bloodstained history of religious conflict incorporates these two qualities of society: All religions consist of those who see "Love Thy Neighbor" as the underpinning of their religion, and have an understanding of the *Erev Rav*, the purveyors of the Death Star fleet, with its energy-intelligence of evil. Accordingly, when one's own religion might be described as intolerant, bigoted, and vicious in the name of the Lord, this represents the manifestation of the antisocial face of the Dark Lord, the *Erev Rav*.

When religious organizations sanction torture, suppression, and genocide, the internal energy-intelligence of evil becomes physically expressed within the cosmos. Religion then becomes a perverting influence, a dark, evil cloud on the horizon of humanity.

From the inner workings of the atom, to the complex surrealism of human behavior, R. Isaac Luria's radical interpretation of our society, and his unique, kabbalistic approach to some of the deeper questions concerning human expression, reveal the fundamental laws that govern the behavior of cosmic forces. Lurianic Kabbalah enables us to comprehend some of nature's most concealed mysteries. Luria's systematic method opens up new vistas of human understanding that were unsuspected only a few centuries ago by providing us with the perceptual tools needed to gain control over most of our existence and even of our environment. Central to his approach is an understanding of the basic questions of existence.

The tremendous power of kabbalistic reasoning is demonstrated daily in the various prayers of the *siddur*, the Hebrew prayer book: "Blessed art Thou, O Lord, King of the Universe Who has not made me a Goy (Gentile)." At first sight, the suggestion seems obvious that to be a Goy is demeaning and shameful. On closer examination of this most delicate issue, however, evidence to the contrary seems to emerge.

"And the Lord spoke unto Israel in the visions of the night and said: 'Jacob, Jacob.' And he said, 'Here am I.' And He said, 'I am the Lord, the Lord of thy father. Fear not to go down into Egypt; for I will make of thee a great Goy (nation).'"[57] Following on the heels of Israel's sin of the Golden Calf, the Lord was determined to put an end to the then existing nation of Israel, and begin a new.

"And the Lord said to Moses, 'I have seen this people, and behold, it is a stiff-necked people. Now therefore let me alone, that my wrath wax hot against them, and that I may consume them: and I will make thee a great Goy (nation).'"[58]

The contradiction is glaring in light of the common derisive connotation of the word *goy* over the centuries. Few would deny that the term, for all its pretensions, has become a negative force in our society. Many people find this expression particularly offensive. And yet, it was the Lord's intent to form a "goy" through Moses. At the same time, the blessing of the prayer comes as a complete surprise. In contrast to the biblical account, the prayer is compelling evidence against the deeper philosophical implication of the verse in Exodus. However, before I proceed to reconcile these two apparent contradictory beliefs, permit me to explore another facet of traditional doctrine, the matter of reincarnation.

In my book, *Wheels of a Soul*, I investigated some of the basic concepts of reincarnation, exploring their implications for society and the cosmos. In most cases, the established ideas of psychiatry and psychology are not so much rejected as they are transcended by the kabbalistic world view. By observing the universe from another angle, the kabbalist has provided fresh insights and new perspectives into the centrality of man and his place in the cosmos.

The subject of cross-migratory souls, as it relates to the topic of reincarnation, has been one usually avoided by most authors. Today, this subject, once considered heretical, is making inroads even into the scientific community which once claimed dogmatic completeness and infallibility. In many details, the kabbalistic conception differs considerably from most, if not all, of the previously published views and opinions. I therefore find myself impelled to perform the modest, yet necessary, task of bringing the kabbalistic perspective of this subject into the light.

In reference to this subject, and for the purposes of our discussion of the goy, I recall a little known section of R. Luria's *Gates of Reincarnation* which describes dramatic changes in the microcosm of humankind. If historical evidence does not always adapt to accepted laws, we must remember that a law is but the result of experience and experimentation. Laws must conform to facts, and not facts to laws. "Laban[59] became incarnated in Balaam, followed by his incarnation in Nabal, the Carmelite.[60] Balaam, the wicked one, drew his power from the serpent, and was called upon by Balak to use his power of the tongue (as the serpent) to curse the Israelites.[61] When Balaam was slain, he became incarnated within a stone, the cosmic intelligence of the inanimate, so that his tongue might be silenced. When he ultimately became incarnated in Nabal, the Carmelite, the process of *Tikune* began, for he (Laban) now reached his ultimate destination, the incarnation into an Israelite.

When the incident of Nabal's evil tongue towards David occurred,[62] and he was intent on cursing David, Nabal remembered his prior incarnation within a stone for the purpose of correcting the energy-intelligence of evil, and he repented.[63]

The process of reincarnation is not so simple as might be supposed. In order to understand clearly just what takes place when a human soul is incarnated, it is necessary to review some of the conclusions which R. Isaac Luria presents on the subject.

"The final incarnation, which was Laban's third time around, now crossed over within the framework of Israel. He therefore became the incarnated soul of Nabal, the Carmelite."[64] Here, for the first time, R. Luria spells it out quite clearly. A non-Israelite may incarnate within the frame of reference of the Mosaic Law. Conversely, an Israelite may incarnate within the framework of the Noahide Laws. Neither framework assures the *Tikune* process. A soul in the framework of Mosaic Law finds the *Tikune* process more demanding and consequently more difficult, hence 613 precepts and not seven."

It follows then that for R. Luria, the *Tikune* process is nothing but the individual responsibility of removing the aspect of *Erev Rav* from the cosmos, whether one is Jewish or not. Having an internal energy-intelligence of either frame of reference determines the extent of the *Tikune* process.

Let us now return to where we started. Within the cosmos there exists the duality of two basic energy-intelligences which originated in Abel: Good and evil, the *Erev Rav* and the other peoples of our universe which are two nations of the world, not determined by any particular religion. Among all nations, religions, and institutions, these two energy-intelligences become manifest. Hence, the term "goy", the nation, represents either of these two characteristics. When good and evil finally are separated, the Messiah will come.

In its original form, R. Luria had, as his main objective, the preparation of the human soul for that renaissance, the scene of "Love Thy Neighbor." He placed the regeneration of the internal self far above that of religious organization or nation as a political entity. Moral improvement would, in his opinion, bring about the delivery of all peoples from exile, as stated in the verse, "And the Lord shall be king over all the Earth; in that day shall the Lord be one, and his name one. And men shall dwell in it and there shall be no more utter destruction."[65] His doctrine of cross-migratory souls imposed upon all peoples of the world the task of *Tikune*. Never before had this doctrine been as illuminating, and far reaching, and pushed to such extremes.

Whether or not one was Jewish, there are those whose souls originated with Abel's energy-intelligence of evil. The only effect religion had upon these individuals was to restrict the extent and severity of the evil inherent in their souls. If they stemmed from cosmic *Erev Rav*, their meanness was without limit. If the *Erev Rav* consciousness incarnated as a Jew, the potential evil and its affect upon the cosmos could be disastrous. The religious consciousness of the Jew is heightened due to the extent and magnitude of his "desire to receive." On Mount Sinai, the doctrine of *Gilgul Neshamot* (Reincarnation of Souls) became closely involved with the conception of the Jew's role in the universe. At the moment of Revelation, the entire nation of Israel underwent a complete transformation.

Adam contained all the souls of humanity.[66] His soul became diffused among the whole genus in innumerable codifications and individual appearances. All transmigrations of souls are, in the last analysis, only migrations of the one soul of Adam. The varied genetic code of humankind depended upon the energy-intelligence of its particular unique aspect of "desire to receive." As in the Endless World, the souls were infinite inasmuch as the degree of the "desire to receive" was limitless.[67]

On Mount Sinai, the Jewish people were incarnated with

souls of the highest intensity of the "desire to receive." This was to enable the Lord to infuse the cosmos with His Endless Light and beneficence. The degree and magnitude of the Lord's power depended upon the capacity of the vessel, the desire to receive this power.

To avoid catastrophic short-circuitry, the Revelation of the Mosaic Law, including the 613 precepts, was necessary to insure that humanity would achieve and demonstrate restriction, the cosmic energy-intelligence of the third column. Without restriction, their unique quality of the "desire to receive" would simply tap the awesome power of the Lord without channeling its beneficial intelligent energy as a circuit. In effect, they could be responsible for violence and destruction throughout the cosmos. The solution and remedy was contained within the Revelation, "Love Thy Neighbor."

The Noahide Laws were insufficient to curtail the degree of their "desire to receive." Only the biblical system of restraint was capable of achieving the fulfillment of man's task in this world if his soul became incarnated as a Jew. The souls of the *Erev Rav*, at the time of the Exodus, displayed the kind of arrogance and insensitivity that marked the failure of their mission. People in our age, lacking compassion and sensitivity, corrupt the entire cosmos with negative energy-intelligence, creating a universe torn by violence and destruction — which is different than the chaos experienced by the generation at the time of the Exodus.

Before proceeding further, I should like to indicate in a few words what I am trying to express by using this much abused term "goy." By "goy" I mean that which generally was meant before the term became a label for a non-Jew. That means that the "goy" signified a concept of insensitivity or compassion, and at the time it became the abomination of our universe.

In this connection, attention must be directed above all to the meaning infused into the idea by two radical situations mentioned in the Bible. This restatement of an ancient conception actually represents one of the most important constituent elements of Lurianic Kabbalah. In all the numerous references to the goy in the Bible, Talmud, and the Midrashim, there is no hint that the term "goy" represents specifically the non-Jew.

"And the congregation lifted up their voice and cried; and the people wept that night. And all the children of Israel murmured against Moses and Aaron. And the whole congregation said unto them, 'Would the Lord that we had died in the land of Egypt or would the Lord we had died in the wilderness. Were it not better for us to return unto Egypt?' And the Lord said, 'I will smite them with the pestilence and disinherit them, and will make thee (Moses) a great Goy and mightier than they.'"[68]

We are obviously dealing here with a special individual characteristic of these people. It is not surprising that the Lord had endured enough of their arrogance. These people were granted freedom, the miracles of the ten plagues, the splitting of the Red Sea, the miracle of the Manna, and all they could think of was, "What have you, Lord, done for us lately?" Ingratitude, of the lowest order, prompted the Lord to declare an end to these people of arrogance and insensitivity. Moses would be the crowning glory of a great goy (nation).

This fact was further proof that with the evil energy-intelligence of Abel, the *Erev Rav*, the Israelites, were incapable of completing their *Tikune* in their existing corporeal bodies. This aspect of Israel continued to remain an essential character of the Jew. Having no choice, the Lord decreed, "Your carcasses shall fall in this wilderness and all that were numbered of you, according to your whole number, from twenty years old and over, which have murmured against me. Doubtless you shall not come into the land, concerning which I swore to make you dwell therein."[69]

"The generation of *Dor Deah*, the generation of intelligence, shall once again rise in reincarnated souls during the Age of Aquarius," declares the Ari.[70] Extinction of this stain of arrogance and insensitivity, and to achieve the doctrine of Hillel the Prince, "Love Thy Neighbor," this is the meaning of *Tikune*.

Everything that is done by the individual or the community in the terrestrial realm is reflected in the upper cosmic region. The impulse which originates from good deeds or from the energy-intelligence of Moses, the good aspect of Abel, guides and infuses the entire cosmos with a flow of blessing which springs forth from the Source, the *Myin Duhrin* of the Lord.

Thus, the Lord, in an effort to arrive at the restoration of the original whole, to remove the fiendish nether worlds of evil, sent Moses, the aspect of Good to be the *Goy Gadol*, the great nation and force, to permit the cosmic seed to fulfill its function.

Toward these *Erev Rev* souls, in whatever religion or incarnation they were destined, was the concern of cosmic Tet directed. She recognized the positive and negative energy-intelligences that ultimately were destined to become physical expressions. This manifestation was what the letter Tet had in mind. The positive energy of the *goy gadel* as represented by the Lord's assurance to Moses, was certain to prevail if cosmic Tet was chosen as the channel for creation. She considered herself the suitable vehicle to assist those souls, incarnated with the negative energy of the evil of the goy, symbolized as the *Erev Rav*, who fall to a lower spiritual plane. For she, Tet, is the first letter and initial energy-intelligence of the Hebrew word meaning good, *Tov*.

A major tenet of the kabbalistic doctrine is that the Lord is One, which, when seen in its totality, means that life and all of its emanations, is basically good. Viewing the cosmos as it emerged from the void and darkness, the Lord said, "It is good."[71] In a monotheistic world view, a persistent problem is to reconcile the existence of evil in its many forms. Anguish and pain in daily human life and natural catastrophes are but some of the physical expressions of evil. These facts must be fitted within the design of creation as it is realized in the course of human history.

The problem of the existence of evil is dealt with by the kabbalist. The willful disregard of the concept of Bread of Shame[72] is seen by the kabbalist as the origin and root of evil and corruption. Consequently, evil did not originate within the framework of the Lord but rather was a direct result of the created being. The removal of light by the created soul brought about the vacuum and empty space that provided the establishment of darkness and evil.

"The Lord saw the Light and it was good. This sentence, in some ways parallels the common perception of the energy-intelligence of sunlight which is generally characterized as one of giving and sharing. The framework of the Lord is sharing and compassion. This stands contrary to the energy-intelligence of evil which is directed by the aspect of the "desire to receive for oneself alone."

The numerical value of cosmic Tet contributed towards her plea to be cosmic channel for creation. Gematria, or numerology, is one of the kabbalistic methods for interpreting the Torah and revealing its cosmic code. It consists of explaining a word, or group of words, in accordance with the numerical value of its letters.

Moses Cordovero explained the use of Gematria in Kabbalah in his basic work on the *Zohar*, *Or Yakar*. Gematria is also employed extensively and is widely spread throughout Lurianic Kabbalah. The works of the thirteenth century kabbalist, Abraham Abulafia are based on the extensive use of Gematria. He recommended the system of developing power of association in Gematria to discover new truths concerning our universe. Many kabbalistic commentaries on the books of the Bible are based, for the most part, on this system, including some which connect with words of the biblical verses via Gematria, thus revealing the mysteries of the cosmos. The Gematria of the entire collection of biblical verses, exposes the immense power of the mystery of the seventy-two names.[73]

Let us, therefore, employ the Gematria in deciphering the internal energy-intelligence of cosmic Tet and its connection with the cosmic code of words. The letter Tet embodies and symbolizes the ninth letter of cosmic Binah, Yesod of Binah, or number nine. Consequently, the Zaddik, representing the ninth decimal letter of cosmic *Z'eir Anpin*, the number ninety relative to cosmic Tet, is the externalization of Tet.

Cosmic Tet portrays the internal, concealed force of Cosmic Zaddik, representing Yesod of *Ze'ir Anpin*, the body and soul concept. The Hebrew words, *goy*, *nehar*, and *zar*, symbolize and encompass the energy-intelligence of most of mankind. The number nine indicates the affinity of those words with cosmic Tet. The internal energy-intelligence of cosmic Tet, consequently, determines the characteristics of practically all humanity.

"The interest of the entire universe would best be served if I served as the cosmic channel for creation," pleaded cosmic Tet. "The Death Star would never undertake any attempt to engage the Lord's battle station, for they could never survive an onslaught by my internal energy-intelligence."

Cosmic Zaddik, the battle station for cosmic Tet, is called "Righteous" for she connects with and augments the forces of Malkuth, the World of Action. Cosmic Zaddik, with Tet's energy-intelligence aboard, was much stronger than evil, arrogance, and insensitivity, the weaponry of the Dark Lord's fleet. With the combined force of their powers, humankind could not fail in battle with the Dark Lord. Any attempt by the Death Star to restore its rulership over the cosmos was destined for failure. Instead, through the power of Tet, the entire cosmos could become a paradise in one clean sweep.

Tet, Cosmic Yesod of Binah, constituted the internal intelligence of Zaddik, Yesod of *Ze'ir Anpin*, the outer space battle station which bears the attribute of Tov (good), indicated by its portal opening at the top of the spacecraft. Cosmic Tet, in fact, is the only letter of the Aleph Beth with a direct connection from its upper structure to the Lord.

This mysterious spacecraft is hinted at by the prophet

Isaiah when he exclaims, "Say ye to the righteous, that it shall be good with him."[74] Furthermore, the mystery of cosmic Tet's awesome power — the concealed Light of the Tet — is that which the Lord subsequently created on the first day of creation. The Sages of the Talmud, alluding to the cosmic power of the Tet, declare that, "this light enabled Adam to see from one end of the world to the other."[75] The bright flame of power ultimately would cast the light of new truth across the galaxies.

"And the Lord saw the Light, that it was good."[76] One who sees the letter Tet in his dream is indeed blessed. Why is this so? The Torah made use of the letter Tet in the words, "that it was good." The letter Tet makes her appearance in this verse. As such, the Tet is considered as possessing the light that radiated throughout the universe from one end to the other.[77] Therefore, cosmic Tet believed herself to be the proper vessel for the creation of the world.

The Lord, however, piercing the curtain of time, foresaw the future. With a view of the wicked generations of the Deluge and Tower of Babel, the Lord now had second thoughts as to Cosmic Tet's intrinsic power of the Light. After gazing upon their evil doings, the Lord decided to hide his light for the future. The light would be revealed for the *Zaddikim* (Righteous Persons), who will appear when the final redemption is consummated. This is revealed in the words, "and the Lord saw the light, that it was good."[78]

Cosmic Tet possessed the force that permitted Adam to see from beginning to end. It was truly an awesome power of intelligence. She was immune to the evil force of the Dark Lord. However, the *Erev Rav*, the *rashaim* (wicked), by means of their corrupt deeds, could crack her security shield, which would place the evil *klippot* of the Death Star fleet in a position to seize the light force.

So long as cosmic Tet remained the property of the righteous, they were in a position to make full use of this power, as Adam had before them. And certainly, if she were chosen to be the channel for creation, the righteous could count on cosmic Tet as part of their arsenal. However, in a universe of free will, the *Erev Rav*, may, as they assuredly did, corrupt the deeds of the righteous. The Bible is full of accounts of their ugly performance. They, the *Erev Rav*, inadvertently would provide the Death Star fleet with the opportunity of seizing the power of cosmic Tet. It was this breach in her security shield which brought about Tet's rejection as a suitable channel for creation, and caused her mere presence within the cosmos to become a symbol of mourning and sadness.

The letter Tet, representing the number nine, has become the symbol for worldwide crisis. The ninth day of the Hebrew month of *Av* brought an end to a world filled with laughter and joy. The Talmud justifies[79] the ninth of *Av* as the major day of mourning. A series of calamities occurred on this day throughout Jewish history. Unfortunately, the violence and disruption that affect the Jewish people has brought pain and sorrow to all nations of the world.

On the ninth of *Av*, it was decreed that the children of Israel, those liberated from Egypt, should never enter the Land of Israel.[80] The First Temple, built by King Solomon, was destroyed by the Babylonian king, Nebuchadnezzar. The Second Temple was destroyed by the Romans. The ninth of *Av* is the date of both destructions. Bethar, the last stronghold of the leaders of the Bar Kokhba war, was captured on this date. The expulsion of the Jews from Spain in 1492 is said also to have occurred on the ninth of *Av*. As strange as it may seem, this day also will see the birth of the Messiah, the beginning of the final redemption.

On *Tisha B'Av*, the ninth of *Av*, the Israelites refused to enter the Promised Land. They feared the powerful nations that controlled Israel, a fear communicated to them by the spies they sent to explore the territory.

"And all the congregation lifted up their voice and cried. And the people wept that night.[81] When the sound of their weeping reached heaven, the Lord said, 'Ye weep not without cause. The time will come when ye shall have good cause to weep on this day.' It then was decreed that the Temple be destroyed on this same day, so it became forever a day of tears."[82]

The biblical book the Rabbis assigned as the cosmic connection to this unique and particular day, *Tisha B'av*, is *Aihah*, or *Lamentations*. The word *Aihah* is similar to the word *ayeka* (where are you) which the Lord cried out to Adam in grief and anger after the sin in Garden of Eden. Both words are comprised of the same consonants; only the vowels are different. These words, as all other words of the Bible, are aspects of the biblical cosmic code. Both symbolize and are connected with exile and represent disaster and destruction. As the sin of Adam culminated in his removal from the center of energy and immortality when he was expelled from the Garden of Eden, so, for the sins of Israel, was Jerusalem destroyed, were the Jews banished from the Land of Israel, and the people sold into slavery and captivity.

In this connection, we must search for the deeper

significance of these catastrophic events of the cosmic disturbances that have shaken our universe. For those satisfied with simplistic analysis, the question as to why the ninth day and not just another day, will be irrelevant. The kabbalist seeks deeper answers to such questions as: Why the ninth day? What is the cosmic force behind this seemingly difficult time period? Why have we been unable to deal effectively with this problem?

Undoubtedly, the connection between cosmic Tet and this peculiar ninth day is quite apparent. It is a universal law that for every power there exists an equal and opposite power. If cosmic Tet's plea to the Lord was based on her energy-intelligence of goodness, then an equal force of negativity must have also existed. The whole idea of duality and free will is part of the cosmic process. King Solomon, concerned with the universal laws that guide our lives, clearly defines for us the essential truth surrounding the essence of creation.

"In the day of *Tov* (good) be connected with *Tov. And in the day of Ra* (evil) consider. The Lord hath set the one against the other."[83] In his interpretation of the cosmic order, King Solomon provided the fundamental cosmic code concerning Tet. Its deciphering emerged as a result of R. Shimon Bar Yohai and his *Book of Splendor*. R. Shimon's interest in astronomy points to a fundamental awareness of the celestial dimension of mankind. Concerning one of the most difficult and abstruse sections of the Bible, R. Shimon revealed the essential consciousness and energy-intelligence of the ninth day of *Av*.

"And Jacob was left alone; and there wrestled a man with him until the breaking of the day. And when he saw that he prevailed not against him, he touched the hollow of his thigh; and the hollow of Jacob's thigh was strained, as he wrestled with him. Therefore, the children of Israel eat not the sinew of the thigh-vein which is upon the hollow of the thigh, unto this day: because he touched the hollow of Jacob's thigh, even in the sinew of the thigh-vein."[84]

The sciatic nerve, together with other arteries and tendons, must be removed from the slaughtered animal before that portion of the animal can be ritually prepared for Jewish consumption. This is a constant reminder of the Divine Providence to Jacob as exemplified in the experience of the Patriarch.

It is a curious fact that although doubt hardly exists as to what constitutes the content of this *mitzvah* (precept), the question I would like to raise about the personal experience of the Patriarch Jacob, from which emerged the foregoing highly mystical precept, is this: Are we to realize its implication simply as an historical phenomenon or consider the experience to be a coded message relevant to our own existence, or can this precept and its influence be traced merely to the fixed forms of dogmatic religion?

The mystical interpretation of the Bible comprises much more than a simple literal translation. Jewish mysticism offers a totality of concrete historical facts, as well as providing an understanding of the Bible's deeper significance. It is connected with, and inseparable from, a certain stage of religious consciousness. A mystical interpretation lies at the root of every biblical precept.

A good starting point for our investigation can be obtained by scrutinizing the *Zohar*, which places emphasis on direct and intimate consciousness of the celestial, metaphysical realm. It is religion in its most acute, intense and experiential state.

"And Rebekah his wife conceived. The children struggled together within her; and she said: 'If it be so, wherefore do I live?' And she went to inquire of the Lord. And the Lord said unto her:

> 'Two goyim are in thy womb
> And two peoples shall be separated from thy bowels
> And the one nation shall be stronger than the other
> And the elder shall serve the younger.'"[85]

What forms the essence of this dialogue, and how it is to be adequately described? This is the great enigma which the kabbalists, no less than the commentators of the Bible, have tried to solve. For it must be said that this drama of a direct relationship between Rebekah and the Lord, between the finite and the infinite, is of a highly paradoxical nature. How can words express an experience for which there is no adequate parallel in this finite world of man?

Yet it would be wrong and superficial to conclude that the enigma implies some inherent absurdity. It will be wiser to assume, as does the kabbalistic view of our universe, that the religious world of the mystic can be expressed in terms applicable to rational knowledge. Therefore, of special interest in this connection is the zoharic interpretation by which we recognize the basic cosmic intelligences pervading the cosmos, good and evil.

"And the children struggled within her, for in her womb

already Esau declared war against Jacob. Observe that the one was the side of him who rides the serpent, while the other was of the side of the Lord."[86] These two goyim were to represent an ongoing struggle between good and evil, peace and tranquility versus turmoil and destruction. The sinister demonic world of evil is nourished and quickened by the sin of man. Evil represents an intelligence making illegitimate inroads upon the celestial realm of light.

This drama of history brings us back to the problem of the sciatic nerve as it relates to *Av*, the most complex and confusing day of the year. What is the basis for this precept? How is this *mitzvah* to be regarded within the framework of the biblical cosmic code? The relationship of mysticism to the cosmic universe can serve as a useful tool for our investigation. For an in depth understanding of this concept, let us return to the *Zohar*.

Why is it called *gid ha'nasheh* (sciatic nerve)? The sciatic nerve contains the power and intelligence to swerve man from the Lord. There, in that nerve, rides the intelligent energy of evil. And because this extraterrestrial intelligence could not find any weak spot throughout Jacob's body, it connected with its primary battle station within man, the sciatic nerve. Consequently, the Torah forbade the eating of this nerve, based upon what the mystics have already stated in this connection. The body of man hints at the extraterrestrial realm. If that body member of man is good, it shall draw the energy-intelligence of good; if it is evil, the energy-intelligence of evil shall be drawn out.

Therefore, when eating the meat of an animal, the intelligent energy of the body member of the animal connects with and is metaphysically integrated with that member of man. For this reason, Israel does not eat the sciatic nerve so that the internal energy-intelligence of the nerve will not be injected into the corresponding nerve of man. Thus, the energy-intelligence of evil is prevented from becoming physically expressed within the cosmos.

Therefore, there are 248 bones in physical man corresponding to the 248 precepts of the Torah. This is for the purpose of providing channels by which the limbs of man may connect to the energy-intelligence of the Lord. Similarly, there are 365 prohibitions of the Torah corresponding to both the 365 varied nerves (the sciatic nerve is one of them) and 365 days of the year. *Tisha B'av*, the ninth day of *Av* is the day corresponding to the energy-intelligence of evil related to the particular intelligence of the sciatic nerve. Consequently, the ninth day of *Av* and the sciatic nerve possess the same energy-intelligence.

It is written, "The children of Israel eat not of the sciatic nerve," with the Bible inserting a seemingly non-essential word " *Et.*"[87] One of the most often used words in the cosmic code, these two letters, Aleph and Tav, reveal the reason for fasting on this particular day. Inasmuch as the prohibition of the sciatic nerve prevents the manifestation of the energy-intelligence of evil from becoming physically expressed, so is there the necessity of fasting on the ninth of *Av*, since the energy-intelligence of this cosmic force prevails and pervades the universe on this particular day. The sciatic nerve symbolizes the expression of evil intelligent energy. So, too, does the ninth day of *Av* represent the manifestation of the energy-intelligence of evil.

The Lord saw all this. The Torah, the cosmic code of the Lord, reveals this through the tale of Patriarch Jacob's

wrestling with the Angel who represented the
energy-intelligence of evil.

"And there wrestled a man with him,"[88] refers to the
year-round struggle of man with all of Jacob's (man's)
physical resources. The intelligent energy of evil could find
no place with which to connect other than Jacob's (man's)
sciatic nerve. This is the meaning of the verse, "And when he
saw that he prevailed not against him, he touched the hollow
of Jacob's thigh and his thigh was strained."[89]

At that moment, Jacob became weak. Similarly, the evil
intelligence found the ninth day of Av during the year in
which he could prevail. The result was the destruction of the
Holy Temple because of man's corrupt deeds and weakness.
This also brought down the cosmic effect of peace and world
tranquility. Those who eat on *Tisha B'av* are likened to those
who eat the sciatic nerve.

R. Hiya said: "Had Jacob's strength not failed him at that
spot (the sciatic nerve), he would have prevailed against the
angel so completely that Esau's power would then have been
broken both on the terrestrial and extraterrestrial realm."[90]

The mystical conception of the Torah, of which mention
has been previously made, is fundamental for the
understanding of the cosmos along with its laws and
principles referred to as the Ten Commandments. The Torah
must be conceived as a vast *corpus symbolicum* of the whole
world. Out of this cosmic code of reality of creation, the
inexpressible mystery of the celestial realm becomes visible.
In particular, the dogmatic ritual commanded by the Bible,
the precepts, are, to the kabbalist, symbols by which a deeper
and concealed sphere of reality becomes intelligible. The

infinite becomes revealed through the finite and makes it more, not less, real. The soul radiating throughout the body puts life into it. Without the Force, reality ceases to exist.

This brief summary provides us with some idea of the profound difference between the superficial interpretation of the Torah, and its comprehension as a cosmic code by the kabbalists. Every *mitzvah* becomes an event of cosmic importance. The energy-intelligence of each precept has a bearing upon the dynamic interplay of the universe. If the whole of the universe is to be considered an enormous complex machine, then man is the technician who keeps the wheels turning by providing fuel at the right time. The energy-intelligence of man's performance essentially supplies this fuel. His presence, consequently, is of central importance since it unfolds against a background of cosmic infinity. By interpreting every *mitzvah* as a cosmic event, the kabbalists gave original and concrete expression to the performance of each commandment. Therefore, a seemingly insignificant *mitzvah*, such as the prohibition against the eating of the sciatic nerve assumes a much wider significance.

Seen in this light, there is nothing more instructive than our comprehension of cosmic Tet. To begin with, Tet embodies and reveals the power that permitted Adam to see from beginning to end. Tet encompassed the wide range of human behavior which included various *goyim*. Her numerical value of nine has found a profound expression in the cosmic effect of *Tisha B'av*, a day of destruction and mourning. The depth of her penetration into the hidden worlds of the cosmos can be encountered at every level. There was, perhaps, no letter more suitable than cosmic Tet as the channel for creation, in that she portrays the Tov (good) that shall exist within the cosmos.

The Lord, however, had something else in mind. "I will not create the world through you, Tet, because the goodness you represent is concealed within you." This is revealed by the Psalmist when he declares, "O how abundant is thy goodness which thou hast laid up for those that fear thee."[91] And so the Lord continued: "This hidden goodness has no place in the world I am about to create, but only in the world to come."[92] Paradox is and always has been an essential distinguishing characteristic of the Kabbalah. All writers on mysticism have laid stress on this point. Cosmic Tet is no exception. She is characterized by two unusual features which may, in some way, be interrelated.

What I have in mind is, first of all, the immense power of Cosmic Tet and its energy-intelligence of Tov, good. Observed by the *Zohar* as a perfect channel for creation, her distinguishing peculiarity of goodness required an extreme defensive mechanism. Hence, the need for her concealment. Her purpose within the cosmic process, despite her concealment, was necessary. All twenty-two letters were instrumental in the establishment of the cosmos. The sum total of these parts, the channel for the embodiment of all its parts, had not as yet come to light. Cosmic Tet required concealment for fear of being exposed to the wicked.

"And being thus hidden within you is proof that your goodness is not destined for this world, but rather for the world to come."[93] Her external, diminished energy-intelligence was ordained for inclusion within the cosmic process, and not the intense energy-intelligence of her essential intrinsic nature. The Lord saw limitation in cosmic Tet.

The initial good of creation was to unseal the soul and untie the knots that bind it. All internal forces and concealed soul energies in man are distributed and differentiated in the corporeal energy-intelligence of their bodies.

Duality and multiplicity shall all appear without duality within the all embracing unity Force of the Lord. The *G'mar Ha'tikune* will then be a symbol of the greatest mystic liberation of the souls. For the present, certain barriers exist that separate the essential power characteristic of cosmic Tet from the stream of cosmic life, a security shield which keeps the Tet confined within the natural and normal borders of the Lord's battle station and protects her against the flood of negativity initiated by the *Erev Rav*, the wicked.

The "seals" which are impressed upon cosmic Tet, protect her against any negative energy-intelligence and guarantee her normal functioning. Of special interest in this connection is the doctrine of Adam's sin and his subsequent banishment from the outer space connection, immortality.[94] What does this symbol represent in kabbalistic terminology? And what is the coded message contained within the "Fall of Adam"? Why were Adam and Eve suddenly conscious of their "nakedness," and why did they sew "fig leaves together"?[95]

In his original paradisiacal state, Adam had a direct relationship with the Lord within the consciousness of *Ze'ir Anpin*. He had what we have been describing as an "outer space connection." Man's origin is a synthesis of all spiritual forces that have gone into the work of creation. Like cosmic Tet, the internal consciousness of the Lord's omnipotence is reflected in his organism. Originally, he was a purely spiritual energy-intelligence. The ethereal shape that enclosed him conformed to the pure naked raw energy intelligent thought of the Lord. Adam's state of consciousness was within the cosmic realm of *Ze'ir Anpin*. At this level of consciousness, Adam was immortal.

It is to the sin that Adam owes his corporeal existence. Born from the pollution of all physical matter by his connection to the Tree of Knowledge, he thereby severed the immediate relationship between man and the outer-space connection. Before this, Heaven and Earth were of one thought and in perfect harmony. The wellsprings and the channels through which everything in the higher celestial region flows into the lower realms, still were active, complete and thoroughly compatible. The vessel (man) and the Force were still in perfect tune with each other. When Adam sinned, the cosmic thought connection was severed. The order of things was turned into chaos. The Force was simply too hot to be handled. Raw, naked energy of this intensity was not meant for our world of action.

The outer-space thought process was over and above the limits of time, space, and motion. The realm symbolic, with all of its limiting factors, were insufficient to channel the heavenly communication. Consequently, the biblical code continues, "they sewed fig leaves together and made for themselves *Hagorot*," insulated garments by which they could sustain the primal energy-intelligence of the Force — just as astronauts need specially manufactured space suits to protect themselves from the perils of outer space.

It is here that we discover the reason why cosmic Tet was not suitable as the channel for creation. The cosmic intensity of her internal structure was such that a potentially polluted mundane process was incompatible to her intelligent energy which was of an "outer space" dimension. The fundamental reality of the terrestrial realm required that her innermost recesses be concealed so as to avoid chaos.

The doctrine of nakedness now becomes closely aligned

with the concept of the outer space connection. The individual soul retains its own particular existence only in relation to its ability to sustain the energy-intelligence of the Force, just as live or exposed electrical cables serve no useful purpose. When Adam and Eve were cosmically severed from the thought process of cosmic *Ze'ir Anpin*, no longer were they in accord with the place they originally occupied, no more were they part of the dynamic interplay of the whole. Their inability to handle the intensity of the Force left them naked. Their banishment into the exile of a strange new form of existence was a particularly abhorrent punishment, both spiritually and physically. Fig leaves, which provided insulation from the unadulterated energy, were their only protection and salvation.

The remedial properties of herbs have been recognized and appreciated since time immemorial. Lately, we have been diverted from the herbal remedies and the true healing process by the fast-acting symptomatic chemical solutions provided by science, but the use of herbs still continues among certain cultures and communities. The use of herbs is the oldest medical science. Herbs are mentioned in the Bible from the beginning of creation. "Thorns also and thistles shall it bring forth to thee; and thou shalt eat the herb of the field," states the Bible.[96] Herb healing was the first system that the world knew. When Adam and Eve were driven from the Garden of Eden and had no more access to the Tree of Life, they were vulnerable to the polluted terrestrial realm of corporeality. Therefore, the Lord added herbs to man's diet to assist and protect him against terrestrial afflictions of negative energy-intelligences.

The Prophet Ezekiel declared, "that the fruit thereof shall be for meat, and the leaf thereof for medicine."[97] These are the Lord's remedies, necessary for mundane existence.

Originally, everything was expressed as a unified intelligent energy whole. Everything was interconnected and interrelated. Only the "sin" caused a severance from the Lord's omnipotence, the result of which led to the loss of the original unified whole and to the appearance of an isolated, fragmented creation of existence. All creations encompassed and embodied the energy-intelligence of immortality, the outer space connection.[98] The universe, then, was one indivisible, dynamic whole whose parts were intrinsically interconnected and could be comprehended only as a pattern of thought in the grand cosmic process.

In the realm of the outer space connection, one never defines entities or concepts as "things." One deals always with the interconnectedness of the thought process. Within cosmic *Ze'ir Anpin*, nature appears as a complicated web of thought relationship between the various parts of an all embracing unified whole. But for the intervention of evil, the universe would never have assumed a fragmented, material form.

The threat of nuclear war is the greatest danger facing humanity today. This awesome power is the result of a process in which the uranium nuclei are broken into fragments. In effect, man has been instrumental in shaking the very foundation of unity within our universe. What are the components of an atom if not thought? The creation of a fragmented atom has led to a profound environmental imbalance generating numerous symptoms of ill health and ill will. The division of the atom is precisely the disrupting scenario created by the sin of Adam. He, too, created a division between the realm of cosmic *Ze'ir Anpin* and the energy-intelligence of this world, Malkhuth.

If the internal energy-intelligence of cosmic Tet were seized by the wicked, the result would be a holocaust far more disastrous than any nuclear war. Therefore, cosmic Tet could not become the channel for creation. The time for her intelligent energy to emerge was destined at *G'mar Ha'Tikune*, the Final correction. Cosmic Tet's dimension in her concealed state was "insufficient to correct this world, Cosmic *Z'eir Anpin* and *Nukvah* (Malkhuth). As a result of this inadequacy, Cosmic Tet would be an easy mark for an onslaught by the Death Star fleet.[99]

The Lord continued: "Furthermore, your concealment was the reason for the Gates of the Holy Temple disappearing into the ground." [100] This was to avoid seizure by the Romans (the physical expression of the Dark Lord's fleet), hence their concealment in the ground.[101]

Cosmic Het, apart from her intrinsic importance within the scenario of creation, also acted as a counterbalance to cosmic Tet. As such, she was poised and appeared as companion to the energy-intelligence of cosmic Tet. We have already noted that all twenty-two letters symbolized and represented the manifestation of the Lord's force, and this included cosmic Het. Hence, they are closely aligned with the Lord's thought-intelligence.

Let us examine Het's peculiarity as a counterforce to the intense power of the Tet. Why and how did Het portray this duality? As Resh and Koof before her, Het served a dual purpose within the cosmos. Het represented the energy-intelligence of cosmic Hod, which corresponds to a left channel endowed to the cosmos by Yesod. Cosmic Tet serves as the right channel, a cosmic embryo by which the souls are brought to birth. The left channel serves to excrete waste to the *klippot* and is indicated by cosmic Het. Het is identified with cosmic Koof because the latter resides, like Het, within Yesod. Yesod is the celestial intelligent energy that provides the entire cosmos with each particular intelligent energy necessary for its existence. As mentioned previously, the portion of energy reaching the Death Star fleet is furnished by the Koof.

Hence, Het, like Koof, appears sometimes as an entity of the Lord's twenty-two intelligent energies and at others in the service of the Dark Lord. This dual nature within the creating framework of constant opposing powers takes the form of good and evil.[102]

While cosmic Het served the cosmic process in creation,[103] she nevertheless undertook the task, "to excrete to the Death Star the waste." These two channels, Het and Tet, are separated only by a very thin wall similar to the layer of the skin which clothes garlic.

The male sex organ, similarly, consists of these two intelligent energy-forces, the life intelligent force of the sperm and the excretion of the urine. Cosmic Tet is the intelligent energy channel that bridges souls from prior lifetimes into the present. I indicated Tet's unique ability to unite the past and the future in providing Adam with an all pervasive view of the universe, from the beginning to the end. *Transpermia*, the term coined by the famous discoverer of DNA, Dr. Francis Crick, is, in reality, cosmic Tet's intelligent energy force which provides the physical expression of an incarnated soul along with its DNA. Tet joins the past with the future.

Cosmic Het serves the Death Star and *klippot*. It is

therefore not by chance that when pronouncing the letter Het, the letter Tet combines with Het in its pronunciation. Additionally, the letter Het expressed, reveals and symbolizes the concept of and word for sin, consisting of the two letters Het and Tet. The Hebrew word for *sin* incorporates these two letters.

The left channel is sometimes capable of gaining dominance over the right channel. For precisely this reason, the male organ also has been employed for evil purposes such as the rape of women. The result of this dominion causes the two letters to combine as one unit in Het, sin. The numerical value of cosmic Het and Tet is seventeen, which is the same value for Tov (good). This implies that good and evil stand one against the other. King Solomon indicated this startling phenomenon when he declared, "The Lord also hath set the one against the other."[104] So when the right channel, where cosmic Tet is lodged, gains dominance over Het, the scale is tilted in favor of Tov. On the other hand, when the left channel dominates over Tet, the energy-intelligence of Tov is subdued by Het, sin.

This, too, is why the Lord cautioned cosmic Tet not to request that her channel serve as the creative process. Her presence would give *klippot* of the Death Star fleet the power and opportunity to tap the Force of the Lord for themselves. Thus, if man corrupted his way, the power of the cosmic Tet would eternally come under the dominion of the Dark Lord.

In this connection, it is worth noting the two coded words under consideration, Tov and Het. Deciphered, they incorporate the entire dialogue between the Lord and the two respective cosmic channels concerning the cosmic process of creation. The word Tov consists of three letters, Tet, Vav, and Beth. Numerically, and collectively, they add up to seventeen. Inasmuch as Tet is the first, and head of, this channel of letter-energy, she therefore is in a position of dominant, primary power. The secondary and tertiary letters of the energy channel of Tov are Vav and Beth, which have the same numerical value of eight, as Het, sin. Consequently, when cosmic Tet gains dominance over Het, the result is Tov, good, for the reason that nine precedes eight.

Conversely, the word Het (sin) consists of two letters, Het and Tet. Numerically, this word channel also adds up to seventeen. However, in her coded position, cosmic Het indicates her dominant position over cosmic Tet. The consequence of Tet's capitulation is sin. Inasmuch as Het is the first letter and source of this word channel of energy, hers is one of a dominant position. The secondary letter of cosmic sin is the letter Tet. Eight precedes nine and the result is contrapositive to Tov.

If there is hatred, violence, and disorder among human beings, it is because there is violence, self-hate and disorder among the fragments of oneself. We permit the Dark Lord the right of entry by our selfish "desire to receive for oneself alone." Why do things happen to me? Because the "me" has become aligned with cosmic Het. Our actions are counterproductive to Tet or Tov. Our primary process, the matrix of our desire to receive for oneself alone makes of us our own worst adversary.

Most of us are trapped in our self-centered cosmic egg that severely limits our human potential. It is difficult to accept the notion that when we want we must share.[105] To receive Tov, one must share and give to others. This contradiction shapes our perceptions of all things around us.

When sin or Het is the primary process for our energy-intelligence, then we exclude the Tet or Tov from our cosmic system. Bad things happen to us because we let them happen. To perceive Het (sin) as a reality instead of as illusory is to dwell in a contradiction.

For this reason, states the *Zohar*,[106] the letters Het and Tet are not found in the names of the twelve sons of Jacob. By this omission, the biblical code indicated that the tribes stem from a higher and more concealed level of consciousness. They were thus separated from the Het, which is a primary source for negativity.

In this connection, the sages of the Talmud[107] allude to the fact that, "the bed of Patriarch Jacob is perfect." This meant that the energy-intelligence of a negative nature never came forth from Jacob to the Dark Lord. This was not so in the circumstances surrounding the two Patriarchs Abraham and Isaac.

Cosmic Tet, upon hearing the Lord's reply understood the decision she would so painfully have to make. She realized the opportunity of the Dark Lord if humankind were to corrupt her channels in the cosmic process of creation. Having no other choice, she departed.

Cosmic Het made no attempt to convince the Lord of her unique ability to act as channel in the creative process. The Lord's reply to cosmic Tet clearly stipulated the danger of Het's presence in the cosmos. Her intelligent energy, as was cosmic Resh's and Koof's before her, was available when and if the Death Star fleet found it necessary to make a cosmic connection. Hence, cosmic Het's involvement was out of the question.

18

The Letter Zayin

Let man always consider himself as though he were half righteous and half wicked.

(Talmud, Kiddushin)

COSMIC ZAYIN WEIGHED HER OPTIONS. TET, DESPITE HER power, had been rejected. Were the Dark Lord to have seized Tet's power by reason of man's avarice, no chance would remain for humanity to achieve *G'mar Ha'Tikune.* The Lord could not afford to gamble on the free will of humankind. Tet's moment of glory would have to wait until the final emendation.

The odds seemed stacked against the positive aspects of future existence. The Death Star knew all too well the impulse that would impel man's greed and corruption. So long as the desire to receive remained unfulfilled, greed would continue to be an inherent characteristic of mankind. In fact, desire to receive would, of necessity, be a permanent fixture in the world to come, for were humanity's challenge of ridding itself of that evil inclination to suddenly disappear, so too would the purpose of creation, which was to allow mankind free will sufficient for the removal of Bread of Shame.

Cosmic Zayin foresaw man's mad race for acquisition and she knew the tenacity with which he would approach the problem of corporeal attainment. She saw the encroachment and corruption that he would attempt to justify in the name of survival. She envisioned that the vast majority of the earth's inhabitants in the world to come would be seeking to satisfy the desire to receive for oneself alone — which it would mistakenly be believed could be assured through the accumulation of material wealth and creature comforts. She saw it all, and it troubled her deeply.

It was true that the challenge to rid himself of this evil inclination would be too great a burden for man to bear. But, what if some cosmic intelligent energy were to be found that might reduce or even neutralize the energy-force of the desire to receive for oneself alone?

With this view of a future cosmos, cosmic Zayin approached the Lord to enter her plea as the suitable celestial channel for creation. An energy-intelligence which would later manifest as the Holiness of the Shabbat accompanied Zayin, for she who would be the channel through which the Shabbat would come into being.

The universe quaked and light swirled around the Throne. Zayin bowed humbly before the Lord and she pleaded, "If it please Thee, Oh Lord, create the world through me. It is my energy-intelligence by which the Shabbat will manifest. And will it not be written, 'Remember the Shabbat day to keep it holy'?[1] Choose me, Oh Lord, for then the universe will be assured of peace and tranquility."[2]

From the kabbalistic perspective, each of us is an integral part of the grand cosmic design. Whenever we experience ourselves as separate from the rest of the cosmos we perpetuate a dangerous illusion, an addictive myth which can cause us to pursue personal gain and satisfaction at the expense of others and to crave more and more intensely to satisfy the desire to receive for oneself alone. This vicious cycle can narrow our focus to include only petty personal concerns. It can alienate the affections of those closest to us and distort our perceptions, not only of ourselves and others, but even of time and space.

The kabbalist seeks to transcend this addictive inclination by extending his consciousness and expanding the range of his vision to include others. Only then is it possible to experience oneself as part of the infinite design. By enlarging our circle of sharing to embrace all that lives — and according to the kabbalist that includes everything both animate and inanimate — we begin to rise above the physical illusion and experience the boundless beauty of cosmic unity.

Kabbalistically speaking, desire, in and of itself, is not entirely a negative trait. The curse of mankind is not desire itself, but only the negative aspect of desire: desire to receive for oneself alone. Desire, in the sense of striving toward some positive purpose, is, in fact, the very cornerstone of spiritual, personal, and material liberation, and the key to inner peace and security. Even the saintliest of men and women are filled with desire — more desire than could be imagined by those whose cravings encompass only greed and acquisition. Desire, however, becomes an attribute only when it is tempered with an underlying motivation of sharing.

Unfortunately, any review of historical data makes it immediately and painfully evident that the vast majority of people are not motivated by a desire to share. Very few are able to escape from the negative aspect of desire because it requires an attribute for which man's inherent desire to receive for oneself alone has made the human race particulary ill-suited, namely a consciousness of sharing. While a few labor at the monumental task of elevating human consciousness, many more work to lower it — the result being that each step forward on the grand scale of human evolution, is accompanied, as the old expression goes, by two steps back. While it is true that science, the arts, religion and philosophy, capitalism, socialism, communism, ethical humanism, and a host of other *isms*, each in their own way may have contributed to the awareness of certain individuals and perhaps may have even improved the living conditions of segments of the general population, humanity as a whole seems no closer today, and in some respects farther than ever before, from achieving what is, or should be, its true objectives of harmony, freedom from want and hunger, and world peace.

Pitted against the Dark Lord, man has not fared well. Despite concerted efforts to achieve peaceful co-existence, the Death Star fleet continues to maintain discord within the universe. No plan for peace seems adequate to lessen the tension between the nations of the world. War, strife and pestilence still reign supreme.

Human history stands as an indelible reminder of the failure of sometimes good ideas to penetrate the human heart. The precepts of the major religions, for example, have been articles of faith for centuries, yet the benefits of religion pale in the shadow of the horrors of the wars fought in their names. The ongoing holocaust of genocide, global war, mass murder, torture and terrorism — scarcely to mention the atrocities committed by man against the earth and her precious resources — forewarns of a troubling and uncertain future as negative forces continue to emerge from the depths of the human psyche.

That such difficulties persist establishes an overwhelming indictment against all of our cherished beliefs and institutions. New creeds and doctrines seek to account for this, but no sooner are they expressed than humanity again makes manifest some new outrage and we watch in horror as the whole philosophical, political, or religious edifice tumbles like a house of cards. Then, slowly, the quest for redemption begins anew. The excruciating irony of it all is that even with the hard evidence staring us in the face, we still persist in maintaining destructive illusions. Ideas alone will never transform human behavior. Only consciousness is capable of penetrating to the essence of the human condition.

In the light of this perception about the frailties of humankind, cosmic Zayin foresaw that neither religion nor the advanced intelligence of science would lead man to his *Tikune*, a term which signifies the completion of the spiritual process of correction and thus has specific meaning for the incarcerated soul. Cosmic Zayin presaged chaos and violence in the life of man on earth and contemplated its seeming senselessness.

Humanity would be surrounded by laws, edicts, commandments and phrases of morality, yet these would mean next to nothing unless the negative aspect of desire was prevented from ruling the human psyche. Unless that one, seemingly intractable problem could be overcome, the emotions that would drive man would forever direct the cosmos in totally incomprehensible ways.

Cosmic Zayin recognized that violence and disorder were the Dark Lord's objectives, and that he was indeed a formidable adversary. The solution, as she saw it, was to impregnate the cosmos with a positive energy-intelligence sufficient to reduce the unlimited needs of the desire to receive. No greater, more all-encompassing goal could be found than to establish a universal system of sharing which would cause man to contemplate his individual responsibility to the cosmic unity.

When the force of *Menuha* (tranquility) can begin to articulate itself as a positive force in the world, it will be largely through the intelligent energy of cosmic Zayin. She alone symbolizes the channel by which Israel, in observance of the Shabbat, pervades the universe with *Menuha*. The intelligent energy of Zayin, portraying the concept of tranquility, is coded in the verse, "*Zahor* (remember) the Shabbat day and keep it holy."[3] The first letter of this precept is Zayin, indicating her ability to provide the universe with a much needed taste of her cosmic energy-intelligence.

In this connection, attention must be directed above all to the meaning infused into the idea of Shabbat by the Kabbalah. Its restatement of an ancient concept actually represents one of the most important constituent elements of the kabbalistic world view.

The etiology of Shabbat is given in Genesis,[4] although the name of the day does not appear there. The Lord worked six days at creating the world and on the seventh day He ceased his work. He blessed the day and declared it holy. A special status of the seventh day and its name were disclosed to Israel in the episode of the manna. The Lord provided manna for five days. On the sixth, a double portion was given to last through the seventh day, since no manna would appear on the seventh day. Thus the Israelites were instructed that the seventh day was "a Shabbat of the Lord," which they would observe by refraining from their daily food-gathering labor.[5] The fourth commandment of the Decalogue, the Ten Commandments, generalizes the lesson of the Shabbat and the prohibition against work on that day. The association of the Shabbat with creation indicates the fundamental reasoning of Shabbat. The sanctity of the day is grounded in the Lord's cessation from work.

The first question that naturally arises is how can we comprehend the concept of the Lord's work? Is the Lord's work in any sense similar to our own? Why should we rest on Shabbat? No human being, after all, has labored quite so hard as would be required to create the cosmos. Could the Lord's requirement of rest be based upon the fact that He toiled too long and hard at creation?

Many religions incorporated the religious experience of the Israelites when they adopted the Jewish tradition that is linked to periodic holy days of rest. When properly understood, the observance of the festivals like that of Shabbat can provide a heightened spiritual awareness to both the Jewish and to the non-Jewish consciousness. The purpose of the biblical precepts and commandments is not to tyrannically regulate behavior, but to add meaning to life by revealing and eliciting the beauty and power of creation through the biblical code of the universe.

Religion, as it is conventionally misunderstood, does little to alleviate the problems of daily life. If anything, it appears to represent a restrictive and stifling system of behavior. With this in mind, of course it only stands to reason that religion is widely perceived to be an impediment towards the enrichment of one's goals and ideals. Accordingly, the vast majority of mankind derives scant benefit from the biblical precepts. Nor is it a surprise that the Shabbat, as it is commonly perceived and practiced, contributes little or nothing toward the elimination of man's inhumanity to man.

Concerning the sabbatical mandates, the fundamental requisite, in the kabbalistic view, is to reinterpret the significance of the festivals and make their meaning relevant and experiential. The story of the redemption from Egypt, which is the traditional foundation of the Passover holiday, is an occasion for stressing man's relationship with the cosmos.[6] The Passover festival directs our attention to the need of drawing upon the Force of the Lord's energy-intelligence.

The sages were eloquent on the value of observing Shabbat. "If Israel keeps one Shabbat as it *should* be kept, the Messiah will come." They say that Shabbat is equal to all the other precepts of the Torah.[7] The Lord said to Moses: "Moses, I have a precious gift in My treasury whose name is the Shabbat and I want to give it to Israel."[8]

Included in the biblical description of the six days of creation is a passage, "and there was evening and there was day."[9] This verse is omitted for the seventh day, the Shabbat. The Bible states in this connection, "And on the seventh day the Lord finished His work which He had made." Thus, the scripture acknowledges that the Lord did work on the seventh day, but it is unclear as to what was created.

What seems to emerge from the foregoing is the idea that the concept of Shabbat has no direct connection with the aspect of rest.

Kabbalah teaches that the seven days of the week are reflections of the seven original days of Biblical creation. Each day represents one of the seven *sfirotic* energy-intelligences by which the cosmos are governed. The cosmic frame of Shabbat is independent of the desire to receive for oneself alone. Man, given the opportunity of free choice, can readily merge with Shabbat consciousness and disconnect from the energy-intelligence of that negative aspect of desire.

This is precisely what was meant when the Lord said to Moses, "I have a precious *gift* in my treasury whose name is the Shabbat." A gift indicates something we receive without effort. Shabbat was a gift inasmuch as the flow of energy was forthcoming without any effort of restriction. On Shabbat, the universe would benefit from an endless flow of energy and desires were to be fulfilled without the necessary restriction. By contrast, the other six days constituted an experience filled with uphill battles between opposing forces, with man acting as the balancing factor.

Realistically speaking, the majority of the Jewish people are not in accord with the Shabbat, nor do they experience it as a precious gift. For many, its observance does not provide the spiritual elevation that such a gift should provide. In the kabbalistic tradition, however, the observance of Shabbat, with the aid of methodical meditation, stimulates the harmonious movement of pure thought-intelligence, resulting in a lingering sensation akin to that of listening to the most exquisite musical harmonies.

The list of works forbidden on Shabbat by traditional Judaism encompasses only those activities that stimulate negative energy. Thus, the labor of a waiter whose job, by its very nature, is designated to serve others, is not proscribed, but if the air-conditioner accidentally were to be turned off on a hot, sticky Shabbat in August, to turn it on again would violate the Shabbat even though little "labor" is involved.

The Zohar treats the Shabbat at length because it is the time when the entire arrangement of the order of the cosmos is altered. The implication of evening and day refers to the basic intelligent energies of positive and negative. The six days of creation consist of a constant struggle between right and left. To man is left the awesome task of creating harmony between the two. The job, for most is taxing. For many, depressing. A unification between those two cosmic forces is the result of our efforts in restricting the desire to receive for the self alone. If we fail to harness the left column, we are cut-of from the flow of energy. The six days of the week give us a washed-out feeling.

On Shabbat however, the structure of the cosmos undergoes a dramatic change. The energy intelligence of the left column, the desire to receive, is placed in a motionless state of inactivity. The internal energy intelligence of the left column during the six day period is a necessary link to the circuit flow of energy. However, as in the case of the electric bulb, the negative pole is united with its positive counterpart by the filament that provides the necessary restrictive energy intelligence for a circuit flow of energy. When and if the filament fails functionally, a short circuit is the result.[10]

Similarly, man must maintain an activity of restriction, a central column consciousness to retain a circuit flow of energy. Otherwise, the flow of energy comes to a halt and man becomes drained.

On Shabbat however, we are free of this responsibility. The cosmos is so structured as to include an inbuilt, ongoing restrictive process. The circuit flow of energy is assured without human intervention or participation. The desire to receive for the sake of sharing is self-acting. This was indeed a gift. The doctrine of Bread of Shame"[11] is deemed non-existent on Shabbat. The desire to receive for oneself alone did not exercise the limiting consciousness or energy intelligence within the cosmos. On shabbat, one could receive endlessly without fear of causing a short-circuit — an eternal filament, if you may.

There was, however, one condition that might upset the Shabbat structure of the cosmos. The cosmic frame of Shabbat existed outside the nature of the desire to receive for oneself alone. Man, given the opportunity of free choice, can decide to remove oneself from the framework by connecting and arousing the energy intelligence of the desire to receive for oneself alone. The electron, whose internal energy intelligence is the desire to receive for itself alone, is cosmically inactive on the Shabbat. The Jew alone has the power to alter this state of consciousness. He can reactivate negative energy intelligence, thereby increasing the need for the central column force. The automatic flow of energy is no longer assured, man's needs are no longer fulfilled and the mad race is on. Unsatiated human, with a drive to achieve he things they believe will bring them a life of peace and tranquility, flood the universe. Everyone seems to have what someone else needs. No one has enough. There just doesn't seem to be enough energy around for everyone.

The decoding by the *Zohar* of Biblical creation introduces a complete reinterpretation of Shabbat which involves no connection between the Shabbat and physical rest. *Work*, as understood by the *Zohar*,[12] revolves around the activity of negative energy-intelligence, the desire to receive for oneself alone. The true meaning of rest is when the desire to receive is in a state of fulfillment, a circuitous consciousness of energy, free from stress. What emerges as important after grasping the *Zoharic* interpretation of the Shabbat is the avoidance of any contact with desire to receive for oneself alone. Shabbat allows us to deactivate the central role of the desire to receive, permitting us to set aside, for a time, the illusion of fragmentation that hides the true nature of existence.

Stress is an essential aspect of life. The ongoing interaction between organism and environment often involves a temporary loss of flexibility. These transitory phases of imbalance exist only so long as an interruption of energy has taken place. A circuitous flow of energy transcends dimension; it is subject neither to distance nor time.

Her recognition of the role of stress in the creative process led cosmic Zayin to plead for her suitability as the channel for creation. The energy-intelligence she causes to become revealed is considered holy because it represents a constant circuitous flow of energy.[13] Under her sway, the universe would be assured of attaining *Menuha*, tranquility, which would result in the negative energy-intelligence of the

Klippot, the desire to receive for oneself alone, being laid to rest. The difficulty in maintaining the quality of restriction, the manifestation of the central column, would no longer pose a problem.

Each of us is a thread in the universal web, and as such we each play a vital role in determining the texture of the fabric of the cosmos. Either we are binding strands, weaving through the cosmos, or frayed, loose ends, disrupting the integrity of the whole cloth.

When the desire to receive becomes neutralized by cosmic Zayin, she becomes a "crown upon the head of Ze'ir Anpin," and the outer space connection is achieved.[14] Thus, the universe once again returns to the tranquil Adamic state of consciousness that prevailed before the original sin. This is the power of the Shabbat. However, this altered state is only temporary because the World of Action, the terrestrial level, has yet to undergo the all embracing elevation of consciousness that will take place at the time of *G'mar Ha'Tikune*.

Each energy-intelligence of the desire to receive may achieve its correction and connection to *Ze'ir Anpin* only when its central column becomes manifest. So long as all its parts retain an element of separateness the six day war, begun at the time of the original creation, will rage on. Only when each and every energy-intelligence has given up all pretense of isolation will the World of Action, with its inherent consciousness of desire to receive for itself alone, surrender its power and allow us to freely transcend the evil *klippot*.

As strange as it may seem, the sages tell us that we will know when all souls have achieved their *Tikune*, their connection to *Ze'ir Anpin*. It is said that this will occur "when the sun and moon shall be of equal brilliance."[15] No longer will negative and positive retain their individual energy-intelligences. Rather, they shall reunite as interrelated parts of the unified whole and the six day battle between night and day will end. Then, at last, peace between the earth and heaven will be restored.

Until that day there will continue to be a six day cycle of activity followed by a Shabbat of rest. This condition will endure until the final correction of the universe at which time the eternal tranquility of Shabbat will be revealed.

"Your energy-intelligence to rid the universe of greed and corruption through complete rest is as yet incomplete," the Lord told Zayin. Her weekly recycling requires man to wage war with the Death Star fleet, before achieving Shabbat, the energy-intelligence of rest. Cosmic Zayin was, nevertheless, an integral energy-intelligence of the Lord's battle station. Yet, the paradox remained. Not only did she incorporate the energy-intelligence of rest and tranquility — at the same time she was the channel for the energy that has reduced the planet earth to a condition of hardship and despair.

The paradoxical nature of Zayin is not alone within the cosmos. Scientists are confronted with paradoxes in a constant array. The kabbalistic world view points up the reason for and necessity of paradox. If humankind represents and initiates the cosmic rhythm of our universe, then paradox symbolizes the dual nature of man. Positive activity displayed by humans infuses the cosmos with rest and tranquility. Negative energy-intelligence of the desire to receive for oneself alone creates a cosmos of disorder and fragmentation, resulting in chaos. In both cases, cosmic Zayin is the channel for their physical expression. The determinator is man. The letter Zayin makes manifest this paradoxical energy-intelligent activity.

The likeness of a double-edged sword is an apt symbol for Malkhuth.[16] During the six days of the week, Malkhuth resides with Netzah (Victory) of cosmic Z'eir Anpin, the outer space connection. This implies that during the weekdays, Malkhuth becomes a "sharpened sword" so as to ward off the attacking Death Star fleet. *Rumheh D'Kroveh* (battle spear) is an attribute of Ze'ir Anpin. Resembling the letter Vav of the Tetragrammaton, the spear is used to pierce the Death Star fleet.

The Lord concluded: "While on Shabbat you, Zayin, are a crown upon and over the head of Ze'ir Anpin. Yet the dominion of that state of consciousness is only temporary. Consequently, your channel can also serve as an energy-intelligence of warfare and holocaust. The universe requires a channel that can assist humankind to fare better in their effort towards *G'mar Ha'Tikune*."

The Lord, therefore, rejected the plea of cosmic Zayin for she represented the doctrine of paradox. The Hebrew translation for the pronounced letter Zayin is *war* — a far cry from the peace and tranquility she also encapsulates.

With head lowered, cosmic Zayin departed from the stage of the creative process.

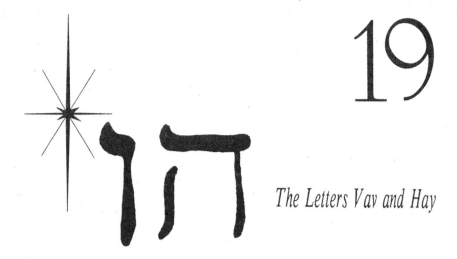

19

The Letters Vav and Hay

God used beautiful mathematics in creating the
world.

— Paul Dirac

Probing the future of the high-tech frontier, the
letter-energies beheld a dreadful vision of the Dark Lord's
Death Star fleet. Flashing like bolts of black lightening across
the endless cosmos, the Death Star fleet left darkness in its
wake, death and desolation. This did not discourage the
letter-energies, nor did it dampen their passion for the battle
to come. Each stood ready to counter the Death Stars with a
defense that she believed would banish forever the Dark
Lord's negativity; each felt worthy of the task of defending
man and the universe against the forces of evil. Yet, however
high and well-founded their confidence may have been,

however firm their convictions, still these factors did nothing to quell their mounting tension. The essential question remained: Who would be chosen as the channel for the Lord's creation, and why?

The time was near for cosmic Vav to present her claim. Examining the pleas of earlier intelligent energies and the reasons for their rejection, Vav found herself hard-pressed to articulate a compelling reason why she alone should be chosen as the channel for creation. Fear did not cause her to hesitate. As one of the letter-energies of the Tetragrammaton, the four letter symbol of the ineffable name of the Lord, Vav possessed power equal to or greater than any of the other letters of the Aleph Beth. In a fair fight with the Death Fleet and the Dark Lord, Vav felt certain that she would handle herself admirably and ultimately fare well. Yet, many letter-energies of considerable merit had come before the Lord only to be turned away. Why, then, should she be chosen? What, if anything, had the others failed to comprehend? How should she approach the Lord? What should constitute the essence of her plea?

As if the universe did not have problems enough — it now seemed certain that violence would be established as a permanent fixture in the human psyche. With desire to receive for oneself alone as humanity's motivating impulse, even a single person's aggressive instincts could be a dangerous force on earth. Sooner or later, man would have to determine what would be the most humane and logical way of dealing with what seemed destined to be in an endless storm of violence and destruction.

Vav's powers of prophecy allowed her to glimpse a future in which humanity would have access to weapons capable of global destruction. She saw a world in which animosity and hatred, the by-products of humanity's violent impulses, would pale by comparison with the devastating radiation and the fallout which those weapons would produce. Why, Vav wondered, would the Lord give man the motivation and the wherewithal to arm himself with enough explosive power to destroy the world ten thousand times over?

The problem, it seemed to Vav, was to find a way of preventing violent behavior from becoming established within the cosmos. One approach would be to limit the amount of violence to which humankind would be exposed. The chosen channel for the all embracing unified energy-force would hopefully be in a position to prevent the destruction of the universe by serving as a strategic deterrent against the Death Star fleet while at the same time permitting man access to the infinite Force of the Lord.

Despite all evidence of the vulnerability of the earlier letters to attack and seizure by the Dark Lord, cosmic Vav still considered herself to be a fitting vessel to act as the channel for creation. As for the single attribute that would qualify her to serve in that exalted capacity, it would have to be her membership in the most elite and powerful force in the Lord's corps of intelligent energies, the Tetragrammaton. With this in mind she approached the throne of the Lord.

"O Lord of the Universe, may it please You to accept my role as the channel in the creation of the world, inasmuch as I am one of the four cosmic energy-intelligences that makes up the supreme Tetragrammaton."[1]

The plea of the cosmic Vav depended heavily upon the exact meaning of the Lord's rejection of cosmic Yood as the channel for the creative process, for she, too, was a member of the Tetragrammaton. If the meaning of the Lord's original vision of a cosmic paradise was an energy-intelligence that would permanently remove the Dark Lord from the cosmic stage of activity, then the power of Vav would probably be more than sufficient to achieve that objective. However, so long as the balance of power depended upon human activity, it seemed certain that the Lord would assure the Death Fleet's survival. Concerning the future only one thing seemed certain and that was its uncertainty.

Even the most ardent and powerful energy-intelligences of the Aleph Beth had to concede that no force then known or foreseeable could guarantee the destruction of every negative energy-intelligence launched by the Death Star fleet. Some part of the Dark Lord's attacking force would penetrate any security shield, causing death and devastation beyond man's imagination.

Perfection, then, did not seem to be the Lord's principal criterion in choosing the channel for creation. Nor would sheer destructive power secure that preeminent post. Slowly, it began to dawn on the remaining letters that perhaps it was a strong defense, and not a devastating offence was what the Lord had in mind. Perhaps it was time to accept the possibility that rather than obliterating the Dark Lord, they would have to be satisfied with a system that would nullify enough of the Death Star fleet to permit humanity the opportunity of repentance and survival. But could a deterrent system be effective on a limited scale?

Cosmic Vav harbored no doubts as to her ability to act as an effective and realistic alternative to man's self-inflicted destruction. The acknowledged threat to cosmic and world stability gave new emphasis to cosmic Vav's internal intelligent energy. Indeed, it seemed that of all the letters-energies who had come before the Lord, she showed the most promise, for Vav harbored a vision of a future world, unified by her energy-intelligence and she was eager to unleash the energy of the central column.

"And it came to pass, as soon as he [Moses] came close to the camp, that he saw the calf, and the dancing: and Moses' anger waxed hot, and he cast the tablets out of his hands and broke them beneath the mount.'[2] The breaking of the tablets precipitated the destruction both of the first and second temples, for the internal energy-intelligence of the first temple was drawn from both tablets, the left and the right, while the second temple drew energy only from the left.

Why, asks the *Zohar*, did the tablets fall and break? They did so because the internal energy of Vav flew out of them and vanished. This power is hinted at in the verse, "And the Lord formed man of the dust of the ground, and breathed into his nostrils the breath of life; and man became a living soul.[3] This is the Vav of the Hebrew word 'formed' which encapsulates the Tree of Life. When Israel emended the sin of Adam, the Israelites were then deserving of the energy-intelligence of Vav, which was designed to create freedom from a world of instability. Thus they earned liberation from the Death Star. However, the sin of the Golden Calf undid their correction and the Tree of Life became concealed. In its place appeared the Tree of Good and Evil. The Torah that Israel then received the energy-intelligence missing from Vav's Tree of Life, which then consisted of life which stemmed from its right side and death which emanated from its left.

This is what the sages meant in reference to the new tablets that Moses presented to the Israelites after the Golden Calf incident. "For those to the right the Torah was a potion of life. From the left a deadly poison."[4] Therefore, the sage R. Akiba cautioned his students to be conscious of the separation and disorder that returned to the cosmos.[5]

What seems to emerge from the *Zohar* is the feasibility of cosmic Vav maintaining universal stability and an orderly cosmos. The advantage the Death Star appeared to maintain over corporeal man and his physical universe, could shift dramatically toward an orderly universe as a result of the enormous spiritual vitality released by an infusion of cosmic Vav's energy-intelligence.

As part of the Tetragrammaton, cosmic Vav had power and cunning sufficient to out-fox even the most deceptive countermeasures the Dark Lord might instigate against humankind. Vav's was precisely the kind of cosmic support that could provide earth's inhabitants with a fighting chance. The Tetragrammaton, the four letter code name of the Lord represented the highest and most potent state of cosmic energy. This was cosmic Vav's secret weapon.

Thus, cosmic Vav asserted, "My dimension of light and energy-intelligence is capable of providing the grand unification for which the universe will one day desperately yearn."Yood, too, had been a part of the Tetragrammaton, but her plea had been steadfastly denied. The Lord's refusal was based on the reasoning that by extending beyond the protection of the cosmic Shin's protective shield Yood became vulnerable to attack by the Death Star fleet — a situation that might have given the Dark Lord the opportunity of seizing rulership over all of galactic space. Should the Dark Lord have prevented Yood from regaining her place within the mighty Tetragrammaton, all would have been lost.[6]

Cosmic Yood's presentation and denial was witnessed at a cosmic conference convened by the Lord himself, with cosmic Vav and all the other letters in attendance.[7] Despite the enthusiasm of cosmic Yood's presentation as the ultimate energy-intelligence capable of defeating the Dark Lord's empire, her plea was declined. Her position within the awesome power structure of the Tetragrammaton provided her with the strength to make such a defeat possible. All of those present sensed the immensity of her energy-intelligence and knew that she was capable of defending the portals of universal space against any dark empire. With the four letter code name of the Lord as her weapon it seemed certain that space could remain a peaceful sanctuary for all humankind. But it was not to be.

The Lord said to Yood: "You are engraved within me, marked within me. My desire and energy-intelligence is in you. Consequently, you are not the suitable cosmic channel for creation."[8]

Vav too was a component of the Tetragrammaton system. For what reason did she believe herself different from Yood? Cosmic Vav's private response to Yood's rejection was to the effect that if Yood's system failed to overcome the Death Star fleet, the entire Tetragrammaton might be jeopardized. Yood was the brain of the system, and if she became corrupted then there was no hope for a universe free of self-destruction.[9] If the Death Star succeeded against the Yood, the entire Tetragrammaton system must fail, whereas the failure of Cosmic Vav, however, could still leave the Tetragrammaton's retaliatory capacity intact.

Vav mistakenly believed that her energy-intelligence, combined with that of Cosmic Hay, could stem the growing dangers that were facing mankind's future. Cosmic Vav felt that as an integral energy-intelligence of the Tetragrammaton system, she could successfully attack the Death Star system. What Vav did not take into account was the fact that she and Hay were as important to the maintenance of the Tetragrammaton as cosmic Yood, and thus they too could suffer the same fate that might have laid in store for Yood. Were Vav to be used in the creation of the world, she would be equally vulnerable to corruption.

The Lord's reply to Vav was, "The Tetragrammaton system in its entirety requires the protective custody of the security shield of the Shin. You, Vav, must not venture beyond its perimeter. Whatever the outcome, the Tetragrammaton must stay clear of any contact with the Death Star fleet."[10]

Cosmic Vav's venture into the cosmic arena would turn outer space into an energy-intelligent battlefield, adding dangerous complexities to the already precarious balance of terror on earth. The overriding issue was the incorruptibility and preservation of the Tetragrammaton system. Above all else, its permanency would have to be assured. If, indeed, the universe were turned into a battlefield of self-destruction, the Tetragrammaton would provide the only hope for preserving the galaxies and the righteous few.

Continuity was the primary thought that hung over the universe and the human species. The Lord had stripped the issue down to a single question: Should the universe with all its inhabitants be permitted to come to an end without the *Tikune* process? The reply of the Lord silenced whatever other thoughts cosmic Vav mighty have had. It was certain that the Lord meant to protect and preserve the Tetragrammaton at all costs.

Disappointed, Vav stepped down from the cosmic arena of selection.

Cosmic Hay no longer sensed the necessity of entering a plea to serve as channel in the creative process. She, too, occupied an exalted position within the Tetragrammaton system. The Lord's reply to Vav brought to her the realization that her energy-intelligence was a vital link in the grand unification of the universe. The young universe could ill afford to gamble on its one certain defense system, the all-powerful Tetragrammaton.

Both Hay and Vav were needed to man this important battle station and ultimately to bring humanity around to the Lord's vision for a stable universe. The Lord's plan necessitated that the goal of world harmony and order be made a centerpiece of His creative process. For this purpose, the Tetragrammaton provided the only hope.

Cosmic Hay, the Lord's obedient servant, had no choice but to also step down and permit the process of selection to continue.

20

The Letters Daleth and Gimel

No point is more central than this, that empty space is not empty. It is the seat of the most violent physics.

— John A. Wheeler

IMAGINE THE UNIVERSE AS A BOARD GAME. THE OBJECT OF the game — call it Galactic Consciousness — is to secure for the universe enough antimatter to bring about the grand unification of the universe. Antimatter, you see, preserves universal balance and symmetry and serves the spiritual needs of the galactic community, but it has a tendency to vaporize the matter which The Technocracy is struggling desperately to accumulate. Hence, it is in the best interests of The Technocracy and the forces of Materialism to rid the universe of antimatter. The rules of our hypothetical game might dictate that human greed and insensitivity, which is fueled by matter, are required in large quantities to feed the specific needs of space exploration and the high-tech frontier. Vast regions of netherspace are completely devoid of antimatter as a result of The Technocracy's efforts, and it is up to us, who battle bravely in the name of Galactic Consciousness, to locate the remaining vital antimatter, protect it, and disperse to those parts of the universe where it is desperately needed.

In recent years there has been an explosion of interest in the scientific community concerning the elusive, ever-present, matter called antimatter. Can it be that there are antimatter extraterrestrials, and even antimatter galaxies, existing in other parts of the universe? Physicists have suggested the possibility that invisible antimatter could account for as much as 90 percent of the matter in the universe. A better understanding of antimatter, scientists claim, might provide insights into the cosmic glue known as the "strong force," which binds together the nucleus of the atom.

It's a jarring notion that the vast majority of matter in the universe might be antimatter. How is it that we find so little evidence of antimatter in this neck of the universe? Logically, if 90 percent of all matter is antimatter it stands to reason that evidence of it would not be so hard to find. Perhaps, in trying to solve the mystery of the missing ghost matter, we might scrutinize the possible reasons for the existence of antimatter.

"One night when Rabbi Isaac and Rabbi Yehudah were sitting up studying the Torah the former said: The Kabbalah teaches us that when the Lord created the world He created the lower world after the pattern of the upper world and made the two the counterparts of each other. His energy-intelligence, therefore, must be both on high and below.

R. Yehuda replied, Assuredly this is so, and that He created man to be superior to all? This is indicated by the verse: 'I have made the earth and created man upon it.'[1] The sages understood the true meaning of that verse. In their wisdom, they translated is as, 'I have made the earth for the purpose of creating man upon it.' I say that cosmic unity depends upon man to complete the organic whole."[2]

This startling, seemingly magical, connection between man and the cosmos is one of many astonishing concepts which the *Zohar* boldly advances. For all but a few scientists, the ideas presented by the *Zohar* represent scientific heresy. Nevertheless, science provides no definitive explanation as to why nature rains havoc and destruction upon the galaxies. Despite science's carefully preserved image as a source of immutable truth, most scientific theories are based on fallible interpretations of the given data. For all their pretense and popularity, few scientific conclusions are immune to uncertainty. The question remains to be answered: Who or what lies behind all negative cosmic activity? The *Zohar* declares that the miscreant is man.

While not nearly as devastating, or as widely publicized, as the horrifying quakes and volcanic eruptions of 1985, significant natural disasters are occurring all the time. A search for new theories as to why these catastrophes happen may assist us in locating the source of chaos and disorder.

Kabbalists defend the ancient belief that human beings consist of a mysterious compound of physical matter and intangible spiritual substance. The physical uniqueness of the human form is derived from a genetic code, but the true secret of the individual is a result of divine creation. The quality that sets us each apart from all others is a non-material self which enters during embryological development, or at the time of birth, stays with us all our lives, and survives after our physical death. This "ghost in the body" is responsible for everything that makes us distinctively human.

The human mind has the ability to grasp higher realities than those ever conceived of by conventional science. In its restless need to express itself, the mind only appears to arbitrarily cut the seamless fabric of reality into myriad patchwork segments. However, in an altered state of consciousness, the mind is capable of restoring the cloth of creation back to its original pristine condition.

Having previewed the drama of creation, cosmic Daleth and cosmic Gimel made their entrance together on the cosmic stage. They knew that individually their intelligent energy-forces were insufficient to enforce the grand unification of the galaxies, but together they represented an energy-intelligence of substantial power. One glance at *Daleth* provides immediate evidence as to why she, alone, without her companion *Gimel*, might be rejected by the Lord. The Hebrew word *Dol* spelled it out at once. Cosmic Daleth's internal energy epitomized impoverishment.

"They now rose to depart, but R. Shimon said: I have still one thing more to tell you. It says in one place, 'For the Lord is a consuming fire,'[3] and in another place, 'Ye that cleave to the Lord are all of you alive this day.' [4]

The apparent contradiction between these two texts has been discussed at length among rabbinical colleagues and it has been established that there is a fire which consumes fire and destroys it, because one manifestation of fire is stronger than another. Pursuing this idea, we may say that he who desires to penetrate the mystery of the all-embracing unity should examine the flame which rises from a burning candle.

A flame cannot rise save from some corporeal body. In the flame itself there are two lights: the upper one is white, the lower is blue. The white light, the higher of the two, reaches upward while seeming to rest on the blue as if upon a throne or a pedestal. The two are inseparably connected, the white resting and being enthroned upon the blue. The blue base, in turn, is attached to the wick, which is attached to the wax beneath it, which feeds the flame and impels it to hold up and cling to the white light above. The blue light sometimes turns red, but the white light above never changes color.

The above is understood by kabbalists to indicate that the lower energy-intelligence consumes anything which is below it or with which it is brought into contact, but the higher intelligence does not consume that which is beneath it. Thus, the energy-intelligence of blue, or black (the effect of combustion), is associated with destruction and death.

Therefore Moses said, 'For the Lord *thy* Lord is a consuming fire.' Literally He was capable of consuming all that is beneath Him. That is why Moses said, "*thy* Lord and not *our* Lord," because Moses was in the white level of consciousness which does not consume or destroy. The white light's energy-intelligence is symbolic of the Force of the Lord. Thus, the ascending flame symbolizes the highest mysteries of wisdom.

Rabbi Shimon continued: The second *Hay* of the Tetragrammaton is the blue or black light which is attached to the *Yud*, *Hay*, *Vav*, which are the white lights of energy-intelligence. Sometimes this blue light is not the letter *Hay* but contains the energy-intelligence of the letter *Daleth*. That is to say, when Israel does not cleave to or connect to the internal energy-intelligence of the white light from below so as to make the blue light burn and cling to the white light, then the energy-intelligence of the blue light is a source of destruction. It is Daleth. However, when Israel is connected to the internal energy-intelligence of the white light (the sharing consciousness), the blue light is then considered *Hay*. Where male and female (the negative energy-intelligences of the desire to receive) are not united and unified as a one basic whole, the letter *Hay* is eliminated and only the energy-intelligence of the letter Daleth remains."[5]

This startling revelation in the *Zohar* concerning the candle is only now beginning to be understood by physicists. In fact, internal energy-intelligence theories have the potential to illuminate many of the mysteries of physics. They are capable of explaining and encompassing everything from the human psyche to Saturn's mysterious radio emissions. Perhaps more importantly, theories built around this concept might one day revolutionize science and our understanding of matter in ways more profound than the leading physicists have ever before imagined.

Daleth's potential for aiding in the establishment of the grand unification was obvious. In essence, without her internal negative energy-intelligence, the Force could not manifest — a situation comparable to a seed not becoming physically expressed without earth, or a flame not being able to manifest without a candle.

Nevertheless, cosmic Daleth was fully aware that her own

particular energy-intelligence was "impoverished." She did not act as an energy-intelligence channel for the Force of the Lord. Nor did cosmic Gimel possess the power to act alone as a channel for creation. Consequently, they decided to approach the concept of creation from a fresh perspective. No letter-energies had ever before contemplated the idea of a dual channel for the creative process.

Cosmic Daleth and cosmic Gimel began with the accurate assumption that symmetry would be an essential property of the world to come. Thus any unified cosmology would exhibit a dual nature of opposing forces. As manifestations of the two fundamental forces in the creative mechanism, they considered themselves capable of bringing an end to fragmentation and disunity. United, they could assist humanity toward the ultimate goal of completing the *Tikune* process, which would, they believed, automatically nullify the power of the Dark Lord and his Death Star fleet — divided they would fall.

The universe is actually much simpler than outward appearances lead us to believe. In fact, everything physical and non-physical can be reduced to an absurdly simple formula which can aptly be described by the two words, *give* and *take*. Oriental philosophy describes this phenomenon in terms of the female principle, *Yin* and the male principle, *Yang*. Science calls it the positive and negative polarities. Kabbalah calls it, Desire to Receive for the Sake of Sharing and Desire to Receive for Oneself Alone. Cosmic Gimel and Cosmic Daleth symbolize this unity of opposites, Gimel representing the positive giving aspect, Daleth symbolizing the negative dimension of receiving.

Actually, in the grand scheme of things, Daleth and

Gimel were not distinct entities at all, but merely separate manifestations of the same underlying interaction, the all-embracing unified whole — which is precisely why Daleth and Gimel perceived themselves as a perfect duet for the creative process, and why they felt confident that together their unified energy-intelligence was capable of initiating the great unification.

The *Tikune* process demands that humanity remain central to the unification of the galaxies.[6] At the same time it is possible for man's consciousness to intervene and disturb the harmony of the universe.

"Cosmic Daleth is considered to be the *Delet* of the Holy City of Jerusalem. When the energy-intelligence of mercy which is the Gimel, the doer of good deeds, becomes united with Daleth, symbolic of impoverishment, Daleth then undergoes a transformation and becomes *Delet*, the gateway and door to both vital energies of the unification process, the Light of Mercy[7] and the Light of Wisdom."[8] This concept of the Daleth acting as a gateway is stated in the verse,[9] "Open to me the gates of righteousness."[10]

While cosmic Daleth, comprised of the three *Hebrew* letters Daleth, Lamed and Tav, indicates impoverishment, when united with cosmic Gimel, the vowel *a* of Daleth becomes transformed by the vowel *e* and is now considered a *Delet*, a door, a gateway to the two great and important lights or energy-intelligences that make up the grand unification, the Lights of Wisdom and Mercy.

The Talmud emphasizes this idea when it states, "the shape of the letter Gimel in Biblical script has the foot pointing forwards."[11] This implies that everyone should step forward and assist the poor. The Daleth, on the other hand, has its upper section extended outward indicating the necessity for the poor to permit themselves to be available for the sharing by the well-to-do. Each complements the other, with no distinction between the two. There can be no sharing without an energy-intelligence of receiving.[12]

If the energy-intelligences of each of the single cosmic letter-energies failed to meet the Lord's requirement, Daleth and Gimel reasoned that perhaps then the galaxies and their extraterrestrial intelligences might fare better with a dual effort to defeat the Death Star fleet.

Some physicists make the bleak prediction that the world will end in an implosion, a Big Crunch, the antithesis of the Big Bang. However, this assumes that there is nothing special about man's place in the creative process. The *Zohar*[13] states otherwise. The *Zohar* maintains that the nature of invisible matter, which consists of pure energy-intelligence, ultimately will warn us if the universe is on the brink of collapse. The thought activity of humankind, in the final analysis, will determine if we will or will not survive.

The fate of life on earth hinges entirely on the state of the metaphysical energy-intelligence of humanity. Depending on the level of consciousness to which we have ascended (or descended) civilization may be destroyed in a fiery apocalypse that will dwarf anything ever imagined in science fiction, or our galaxy may be spared and never have to face up to the prophecy of cataclysm.

Towards the prevention of the final crunch, under the assault of the Death Star fleet, cosmic Daleth and cosmic Gimel bent their attention. They were certain they could provide sufficient energy-intelligence to prevent the overthrow of the universe by the Dark Lord. With this in mind, they approached the Lord.

"Hear our plea, Oh Lord, for we are most desirous of being chosen as the dual channel for creation. Together we represent an aspect of the power of balance and symmetry. Thus, we could generate enough central column energy to thwart any massive attack on the cosmos by the Death Star fleet."

While cosmic Daleth's battle station was located well within the Lord's security shield, the Death Star fleet could gain access to her internal force. If the shield were penetrated, the Lord's kingdom would remain in eternal jeopardy. Daleth's problem was similar to that of cosmic Shin. The corner of the roof of cosmic Daleth's spacecraft, protruding with the light energy-intelligence of Hesed (Mercy),[14] provided the Death Star fleet with the opportunity to plan its attack on the unsuspecting Daleth, and possibly inflict a breach in her connection with cosmic Gimel. Thus Daleth's link with the Force (Light of Wisdom) could become severed and the Death Star fleet could neutralize her internal energy-intelligence.

Once the Dark Lord gained access to the energy-intelligence of the Daleth, he would be capable of forging her likeness with that of cosmic Resh. By severing Daleth's antenna link (the right upper corner) her spacecraft could be transformed to resemble Resh (poverty). Daleth's capture by the Death Star fleet would thus provide the Dark Lord with another spacecraft to add to his Death Star fleet.

Before the fall of Adam and the subsequent shattering of

the vessels, Koof and Resh maintained a perfect unification and symmetry of interactions. Only following the first disruption within our universe did the Dark Lord find his opportunity to manifest severely negative intelligence. Despite the efforts of Koof and Resh, the balance of power rested on the side of the Death Star fleet.

Were the universe to be created through Daleth, there would always be a danger of the Death Star seizing ultimate control. Empty space could be reduced to a vast wasteland of static negative intelligence, a condition which most certainly would trigger such diverse calamities here on earth as earthquakes, human illness and drought.

Although geologists comprehend the action of plate tectonics perhaps better than any other aspect of the earthquake-generating process, the greatest remaining mystery is why earthquakes happen at all. The key to solving this mystery lies in isolating the cause that arouses the geologic imbalance that makes the earth's crust change position. Seismologists have no way of knowing precisely when one geologic plate will break free of another and set the earth's crust crumbling. According to the *Zohar*[15], the answer to the mystery is to be found in the hot, turbulent atmosphere of Malkhuth, the illusory space where the forces of the Lord, supported by positive human activity, wage battle with the Dark Lord, assisted by negative human activity.

"One day R. Yehudah fell asleep under a tree and dreamt that he saw four spacecraft outstretched and Shimon Bar Yohai ascending on them with a scroll of the law, and also with all manner of books containing all the hidden secrets and mysteries of the universe and *agadot*. They all ascended to heaven and were lost to his view."[16] Bar Yohai's journey to

Malkhuth consciousness in the second century began when he fled from the Romans to a cave in P'quiin.

Consequently, in the Lord's reply to Daleth and Gimel, He stated, "My cosmic letter armada could ill afford the loss of any lettered spacecraft, especially one so valuable an ally as you, Daleth."

Daleth, makes herself available to persons of means so as to permit transfers of energy from the rich to the poor. Thus, she is responsible for the establishment of "circular concept," a complete circuit of energy. Without her cosmic function, humanity could not make manifest the internal energy-intelligence of benevolence, for without the impoverished, the rich could not genuinely share. If Daleth became poorer (Resh) by reason of her being deprived of light of Hesed, (Mercy), the opportunity for chaos and disorder would be vastly increased, which would pose a threat to the very balancing mechanism of the universe.

"You two must remain side by side," said the Lord, "since it is written, 'the poor shall not cease from the land.'[17] Stay side by side together as you both need extraordinary precautions to avoid seizure by the Dark Lord."[18]

By virtue of their internal energy-intelligence, Daleth and Gimel provide the metaphysical space systems by which earthbound humanity, through the activity of sharing and receiving, as demonstrated by the rich and poor, maintain balance and harmony in the cosmos. "As above, so below."[19]

Together, Cosmic Daleth and cosmic Gimel departed from the presence of the Lord.

21

The Letter Beth

*Still there are moments when one feels free from
one's own identification with human limitations
and inadequacies. At such moments, one imagines
that one stands on some spot of a small planet,
gazing in amazement at the cold yet profoundly
moving beauty of the eternal, the unfathomable.*

— Albert Einstein

BLESSING IS AN ELUSIVE CONCEPT. IF YOU'VE EVER
attempted to describe it you have probably fumbled
uncomfortably with words such as bliss, good luck, Godsend,
harmony and happiness, and you might just as easily have
been dissatisfied because blessings are all of these and none of
them. Another word that might be used to describe the idea
of blessing is unity. You can't hear unity, can't taste, touch,
or smell it, and yet we can certainly feel when it is upon us,
and also when it disappears. Marriage supposedly depicts the
ultimate unification of two people, and yet half of all
marriages end in divorce. Indeed, it is often said that the

surest way to end a beautiful romance is to get married. How quickly in such instances does a seeming blessing turn into a curse.

If there is one thing about blessings that many people would agree on, it's that blessings have a funny way of ending up on other people's doorsteps and not their own. Blessings seem to rain down on others, but though we thirst for their life-giving elixir, seldom does much more than a drop, it seems, land on us — or at least that is how the common thinking goes.

Blessings depend upon the perspective from which they are viewed. One person's blessing can be another's curse. A bowl of brown rice is equivalent to a king's ransom in the eyes of a starving man, but possibly an insult to the senses of one whose palate is accustomed to gourmet food. Yet serve a steady diet of brown rice to the man who was starving and deprive the other of food and it will not be long before the tables have turned, brown rice falling dramatically in the estimation of the former while rising significantly in the eyes of the latter. There we see how in the space of a few days the blessing-curse dichotomy can completely reverse itself.

Attitude, circumstances, even time, can play a part in the way we perceive blessings. One of the fundamental traits of human consciousness is our ability to perceive the ongoing presence of time. When we see two snapshots, one of a person as a baby and another of the same person as an adult, we have no trouble in determining which was taken first. Time moves inexorably forward. All this seems quite obvious and even trivial until we ask: but does it really? Why should time not march backward, or even sideways? If kabbalists are correct (and also a few brave theoretical physicists) and time-space is part of an infinitely dimensional continuum, why, then, can't we remember tomorrow as well as we can remember yesterday?

The fact that we don't normally remember into the future is no reason to say that we cannot. Many people have experienced prescience and feelings of having been in a certain situation before. Scientifically speaking, of course, things of this nature are impossible. Quite naturally, then, scientists have advanced "rational" theories which attempt to explain away prescient messages as being nothing more than short circuits in the brain. Who, then, are we to believe — the kabbalist who tells us that human consciousness has access to the past and the future, or the scientist who says that the past and the future do not exist?

Scientists are the first to admit that they know next to nothing about the human brain. And nor can they agree on a theory that can explain the forward march of time. According to some theories, time, were it possible to travel beyond the speed of light, could hypothetically run in reverse. And if it were possible to travel at precisely the speed of light presumably there would be no reason why we could not remember next year as clearly as last.

Einstein took notice of this contradiction. In a famous letter after the death of his friend, Michele Besso, Einstein wrote to Besso's sister stating, "Michele has left this strange world before me. This is of no importance. The distinction between past, present, and future is an illusion, although a persistent one."

One of the world's leading cosmologists, Roger Penrose of Oxford proposes that time is purely a psychological event.

Consciousness makes time move forward and thus, presumably, it can also make time run in reverse. A flipped coin, for example, spends half of the time as *heads* and the other half as *tails*. Uncertainty exists even after the coin has landed and been covered with the hand. Psychologically speaking, time expands until the moment the coin is uncovered.

If time runs forward in an expanding situation, such as the point in time when we flip the coin until its revelation and backwards after the revelation, then presumably at the moment of reversal it runs in both directions at once. Does it then snap back to the moment that the coin landed? Is time, then, reversed at the moment of the uncovering and does potential then become reality? At death do we become retropeople?

Of course, all this is hopelessly confusing. And it will remain so as long as we remain ignorant of the illusory nature of physical life and the extreme limitations of so-called "rational" thinking. Only by transcending rational consciousness can we ever hope to unravel the mysteries of our universe and alleviate the confusion that surrounds us in our everyday lives.

Because of the limitations of rational thinking, we have to accept the fact that, as Werner Heisenberg phrased it, "Every word or concept, clear as it may seem to be, has only a limited rage of applicability."[1] The physical universe is replete with paradox. This fact goes a long way towards providing us with an explanation of why so such confusion exists in the universe and ultimately in our own personal lives.

Steven Weinberg, one of the world's leading theoretical

physicists, and co-architect of the "unified theory" of the weak and electromagnetic force, once wrote that the more the universe seems comprehensible the more it also seems pointless. His remark is typical of many made by scientists who conclude from their vast and extensive research that the universe seems to have no discernable purpose and therefore must be considered to have emerged as a result of a vast and meaningless accident.

How can anyone possibly conclude that we live in a cosmos where chaos reigns supreme? Simple observation should tell us that the universe is anything but random. Just take a look around us. Has anything yet emerged that we may unequivocally conclude arose without meaning or purpose or by virtue of an accident? Every advance in fundamental physics uncovers yet another facet of the universal order. Yet, the fact is that no matter how deeply the scientist probes the depths of space and the subatomic realm he will always encounter deeper, more unfathomable mysteries. Nature is too subtle, far too profound to be laid bare by the scientific method.

A few physicists, like Erwin Schrodinger, admit the confusion to which their investigations have led them. "I know not whence I come, not whither I go, nor who I am." Curiously, one of the sages in the *Ethics of the Fathers*, having surveyed this same conceptual construct, arrived at quite a different conclusion than Erwin Schrodinger. "Akabya ben Mahalalel said: "Consider three things, and you will not fall into the power of sin, illusion. Know from whence you came, whither you are going, and before whom you are about to give an account and reckoning."[2]

To the student of Kabbalah, Akabya's three principles

represent the three intrinsic universal forces. These three energy-intelligences, along with the fourth force, man, whose innate intelligence is one of lack or need (desire to receive for oneself alone), combine to control the universe. These four forces are manifestations of a single underlying superforce which ultimately accounts for all activity in the universe.

This unified force could and would maintain stability throughout the cosmos, preventing chaos and illusion from becoming the universe's dominating influence. The superforce, the infinite reality, lies beyond conventional physical experimentation and finite understanding. Only within a metaphysical frame of reference, can man be freed from the world of illusion and gain access to the infinite reality where clarity rules supreme. This was a very powerful philosophical condition that would have to be met if the illusion of a free universe were to be avoided.

Set against this theoretical excitement, cosmic Beth entered the arena of creative speculation. Beth was well aware of the flaws in the reasoning of each letter that had come before her. For every positive characteristic that each one possessed, there was an equal and opposite force within their makeup which would have created a universe of duplicity and confusion. Had any of the previous letters been chosen to act as the channel for creation, the cosmos would have been ruled by blind chance and not by the absolute clarity which governs the real world of the infinite.

The Dark Lord and his Death Star fleet would dearly have loved it had the Lord chosen to create a universe where chaos reigns supreme. But, thankfully, this was not what the Lord had in mind. His blueprint called for a design whereby man would be able to discern, if he would so choose, between the reality of the infinite and the illusion which of necessity would be presented by finite existence.

It was essential to the task of the creative process that man be given a system by which to avoid the uncertainty of a random universe. Such was the nature of the superforce which would always be there to assist the spiritually inclined man in his quest toward infinite consciousness. Free will and determinism would, of necessity, exist as distinct, though interrelated, parts of the cosmic landscape. Thus would the spectacular pattern of the impeccably ordered universal design be revealed, but only for those who understood and exercised the principle of resistance.

The stage was set for cosmic Beth to make her plea. "Oh Lord of the universe, may it please you to establish the creative process through me, for I represent the energy-intelligent force of *berakhot* (blessings), the first letter of the coded force known in the terrestrial realm."[3]

Beth, the superforce, expressed in a word her unique energy-intelligence. Her *Berakhot* could bathe the entire universe with the only energy capable of washing away illusion, thereby enveloping the terrestrial realm with the intrinsic reality of the upper, metaphysical realm. Only the energy-intelligence of *Berakhot* is capable of removing the illusion of corporeal reality and revealing a cosmic model that is, was, and will always be static, timeless and perfectly still. And Beth, as messenger of this intelligence, is the only letter-energy capable of expressing the unity of the all embracing Force of the Lord.

The ultimate truth about the universe, and a proper understanding of the evolutionary process of creation, requires that the mind's intrinsic state of deception is removed through man's voluntary resistance. Superforce Beth assured the Lord, that her energy could pave the way for a new reality in which the old, illusionary mind-set would give way to the all embracing reality of the cosmos.

Beth was the first letter to represent a distinct threat to the Dark Lord. Hers was the first energy with the capability of filling the false vacuum, thus preventing the inhabitants of the physical universe from mistakenly perceiving their corporeal surroundings to be an event without a cause. Were it not for Beth the idea of a free universe might be taken seriously. Of all the letters who had pleaded their merits, only Beth's blessing could allow man to have an internal connection with the absolute certainty of the Force.

Consequently, cosmic Beth pleaded that her energy was necessary to lay to rest the illusionary pattern that the Dark Lord would weave into the fabric of the universe. Otherwise, were the Dark Lord to come to power, man might abdicate his duties of determination of cosmic activity and opt for the free and easy illusionary way out of constant dilemma — although in the long run this would be most painful.

And what was the Lord's response to Beth's plea? He said, "Assuredly, through your channel I will create the world. Yes, your energy-intelligence shall be at the starting point to the creative process."[4]

What is this mysterious superforce of cosmic Beth that when accessed provides clear, definable laws and principles as opposed to an illusionary uncertainty? To appreciate Beth's energy-intelligence let us turn to the *Zohar* which takes the position that only from observation can one ever arrive at truthful conclusions. To many this outlook may seem lacking in faith, but the *Zohar* and the kabbalist simply do not accept the Superforce or anything else without personal verification.

The question of how we can be certain of the interpretation of the metaphysical realm of superforce Beth is carefully considered by the author of the *Zohar*: "And for those persons who do not know, yet have a desire to understand, reflect upon that which is revealed and made manifest in the terrestrial level, and you shall know that which is concealed, inasmuch as everything (both above and below) is the same. For all that the Lord has created in a corporeal way has been patterned after that which is above."[5]

Armed with this introduction to superforce Beth, we can now turn to what is probably the most mysterious and profound development in the understanding of the origin of the universe, the internal energy-intelligence of the superforce which allows spiritual people access to the infinite reality while the non-spiritual sector of humankind, those who surrender to desire to receive for oneself alone, see only fragmentation.

"Everything below corresponds entirely to that which is above. This is the significance of the words: 'And the Lord created man in His own image; in the image of the Lord created He him.'[6] Just as in the firmament which covers the whole universe, we behold different shapes formed by the conjunction of stars and planets to make us aware of hidden things and deep mysteries. So upon the skin which covers our body and which is, as it were, the body's firmament, covering all, there are shapes and designs — the stars and planets of the body's firmament, the skin through which the wise of heart may behold the hidden things and the deep mysteries indicated by these shapes and expressed in the human form. Concerning this it is stated, [7] 'The viewers of the heavens, the stargazers...'"[8]

The scientist may shake his head in despair at such a statement, but once again, the *Zohar* makes it clear that the, "the body of man is related to our entire galaxy and universe." An in-depth analysis of the body, along with understanding which planet or which part of our galaxy relates to each different section of man, the different parts of man will open new vistas to the heavens.

It therefore comes as no surprise that the famed Italian kabbalist, Shabbatai Donolo was also a physician. His famous work on the *Sefer Yetzirah*, known as the Book of Wisdom, explains in precise detail the composites and relativity of one planet to another. His *Book of Remedies* contains a great deal of material drawn from his comprehension of the Kabbalah.

What is it that distinguishes cosmic Beth from all other cosmic letter-intelligences? A good starting point for our investigation is to understand where the coded information sequences might come from. And for this I must again appeal to the profound aspect of the Hebrew letters, namely to their unique and peculiar design and the way they have become manifest. The Hebrew alphabet describes how energy-intelligences of all kinds, desire to share and receive, restriction, travel and pervade through space and their crucial role in all life forms of the four kingdoms.[9]

Their study, therefore, forms an important part of every modern course in all of science. On a cosmic scale the effect of introducing information from the future is far-reaching.

Instead of a universe beginning in a big bang and seemingly degenerating ever since, the perceptive observer of nature can see that a primordial state of affairs can become more sophisticated as time goes on.

The natural impulse in thinking about intelligence in the cosmos is to start with ourselves and then to attempt to work upwards towards the unknown. The path of the kabbalist is to jump straight towards the concept of an all-embracing intelligence. In so doing we have left aside intermediate intelligences that may be masked by the happenings of our earthly existence, a concept of the *Zohar* to which we will now turn.

"R. Hiya said that the Oral and the Written Law together preserve mankind, as it is written: 'Let us make man in our image, according to our likeness'[10] — image having reference to the masculine (code name for the metaphysical realm) and 'likeness' to the feminine (code name for the physical realm): and for this reason the Bible commences with the letter *Beth*. R. Isaac said: Why is the Beth open on one side and closed on the other? To indicate that when man desires connection with the internal energy-intelligence of the Torah, it is open to receive him and connect with him. And when a man closes his eyes to it and walks in the other direction (non-spiritual) then it turns its closed side to him, according to the saying: 'If thou leavest me one day, I will leave thee two days,'[11] until he returns to attach himself to it, never again to abandon it."[12]

What seems to emerge from the preceding *Zohar* is the intelligence aspect that the *Zohar* attaches to cosmic *Beth*, the interaction between man's desire and intelligence and the intelligence of a higher cosmic order, namely cosmic Beth.

Furthermore, it established cosmic Beth as the celestial metaphysical gateway and connection to the all important compendium of energy-intelligence, the cosmic code, also known as the Bible. In addition, contact can be made with extraterrestrial intelligences right here, in our own environment, namely, the twenty-two letters of the Aleph Beth.

Through all of our history we have observed the stars and mused whether humanity is unique or maybe, somewhere else in the dark of the night sky, there are fellow intelligent beings like ourselves who deliberate and consider as we do. Scientists working on the question of extraterrestrial intelligence are making attempts to ascertain whether there are advanced civilizations in the Milky Way. Naturally, any estimate or conclusion is little better than a guess. There is so little known of the origin of life or the probability of the evolution of intelligent life.

The Milky Way Galaxy and its inhabitants, the Dark Lord with the Death Star Fleet has been dealt with in another section of this book. But what is refreshing is the awareness and clarity by which the *Zohar* has dealt with extra-terrestrial energy life forms. Suffice to say, there are no other life forms as earth's humankind. This has already been stated in the *Zohar*.

That extra-intelligence life forms exist as 'energy' life forms was known by R. Shimon. However, the activity and efforts of these forces depend entirely on earth's human behavior and activity. By and within themselves they cannot exercise free will. They are a civilization of robotic consciousness. The power of the Dark Lord and his empire at the Milky Way space station are fueled by man's inhuman attitude towards his fellow man.

I think it is wise, when coming face to face with such
profound mysteries as Superforce Beth, that we feel at the
same time a little humility. With our present understanding of
this vast and awesome cosmos, we know very little. However,
the times we live in are very interesting ones. Questions never
before asked are now subject to inquiry. Therefore, the
Zohar, a body of knowledge replete with so much
information, could not be as alive and relevant, vibrant and
growing, if it were not responsive to the most serious scrutiny
and investigation.

Consequently, the *Zohar* in its attempt to provide an
understanding of our universe and our participation raises
further questions concerning Superforce Beth. Why and what
established the particular design for Superforce Beth in the
first place? Merely to establish Beth as the Superforce of
creation only raised more questions. And since the kabbalist
always asks *why*, no stone shall be left unturned until the
final why is laid to rest.

"R.Judah said: The Beth has two parallel lines and a third
joining them. What do these signify? One for heaven, portrays
Ze'ir Anpin, the outer space connection, and one towards
earth, portrays Malkhut, the terrestrial realm. The line joining
both parallel lines is the Lord, the code name for the *Sfirah
Yesod*, unites and receives them. R. Elazar said: These three
energy intelligent forces represent and symbolize the three
column energy system [13] by which our universe has become
associated with, the three column system in which the whole
of the cosmic code, the Bible, is comprised. Beth is the
gateway and opening of the all embracing Amen,[14] which
leads to the inner sanctum of the Torah. Furthermore, the
word Beth means *Bayit* (house), housing the forces of the
three energy-intelligences, portrayed by the three columns of

letter Beth. Cosmic Beth is therefore all inclusive of the Torah, since the Torah begins with Beth. She is therefore the healer and stabilizer of the universe"[15]

There is one further question that must be raised, and that deals with the idea of columns or the letter Vav which symbolizes and portrays a column. What is the significance of cosmic Beth's structure that seems so crucial to the awesome power of the Superforce mentioned in the *Zohar*. Where did the awesome power of the three column idea originate? After all, what does the power of the atom consist of if not the three energy forces: proton, electron and neutron?

Prior to the miraculous splitting of the Red Sea, an unusual event that has remained as one of the most impressive cosmic upheavals in the long history of humankind, Moses drew the all-inclusive positive cosmic energy force by tapping the source of this energy from the Tree of Life. How did Moses connect to this awesome power without 'burning out'? When and where in the Bible did this secret become revealed?

The secret lies in the mystery of the seventy-two letters. Rabbi Shimon further said that the *Shekhinah* was then in her fullness and perfection manifesting in herself seventy-two holy names according to the threefold order, namely the three columns or the secret of the three verses[16] that each one begins with the letter Vav.[17]

The three verses mentioned in the *Zohar* represent the most powerful evidence that the Bible is nothing more than a cosmic code of awesome power. The three verses contain each precisely seventy-two letters. All three begin with the letter Vav[18] and subsequently became known as the three column system in as much as the letter Vav portrays the dimension of a column. The number three should immediately draw the reader's attention to the significance of the all embracing unified power of Hesed, Gevurah and Tifereth which symbolize right, left and central and also the three atomic components, proton, electron and neutron.

This then, constituted the essence of cosmic Beth's plea. She was a superforce simply because her construct embodied the all embracing unified whole. Thus cosmic Beth could establish "blessings" in the universe, the unification of all the worlds, upper and lower in as much as she embodied, by her structure of the three letters of Vav, the Mosaic code of unification, the seventy-two letters.

For the reader of this book, may I suggest you at least "taste" this awesome power of the universe, the Superforce. How? Turn to Volume Eight of the Center's Zoharic edition, page 311,[19] and scan the tablet of the seventy-two letters. Yes, you will find the Superforce written in the Hebrew letters of the Aleph Beth. And if you cannot read Hebrew, may I suggest that you read the code of letters anyway and I assure you that your subconscious, the real you, the ninety-nine percent of you, shall capture the essence and internal force of the cosmic code of the Superforce. Something will be retained or possibly everything. This will depend entirely on your own level of spirituality and not to the degree of your religiosity.

The greater the degree of your "love for your neighbor," so shall be measured your connection with the Superforce. The more your head trip is in-tune with the sharing-restriction attitude, the more closely will the Superforce become attached to you.[20]

The question that might be going through your mind after reading my idea of scanning the Hebrew words of the seventy-two letters is how in heavens name can a simple examination of letters become incorporated with the inner self?

Well, for those of us who consider ourselves beneath the intelligence of a computer, then we do have a problem. However, if among my readers there are some who consider themselves at least equal to the intelligence level of the computer, then may I make a suggestion. Take a trip down to your supermarket and observe the check-out counter. There you will notice the clerk passing the purchased item over a scanner with the funny looking squared configuration that usually appears on the back facing the scanner. What the observer is told is that the scanner immediately relays this information to a computer which in turn transmits the purchase price back to the cash register instantaneously.

This is precisely the interrelationship that exists between our eyes and our mind computers. The scanning of the tablet of the seventy-two letters immediately establishes the information in our mental software. It is similar to duplicating information from one floppy disc to another. So there it is. If you're not familiar with the Hebrew letters or words, at least you have the opportunity of copying the seventy-two letter software onto your personalized mind computer.

We have now connected with the software program of Cosmic Beth. This by virtue of our "knowing" the structure and embodiment of Cosmic Beth which consists of the three column system. Knowledge is essentially a mental process and knowledge "is" the connection to the real reality. This secret is disclosed by the *Zohar* when deciphering the coded verse,

"And Adam knew Eve his wife; and she conceived and bore Cain."[21] How can the mere act of knowing create a pregnancy? The *Zohar* explains this simply as the difference between information and knowledge. Knowing is the connection. Obviously there was an act of physical intercourse, but that is not the point sought by the *Zohar*. The only time information can become connected with us is when we understand and "know" the information..VDP[- .06]22

To know Cosmic Beth, the Superforce, requires an understanding "why" she is structured the way she is. With that knowledge now behind us, we can now proceed to make contact with the internal energy-thought-intelligence of the Superforce, the Force that motivates Beth's Superforce into the power she represents. The force, the centrality of any channel-communication effect adjusts itself to the capability and capacity of the instrument making manifest the Force.

Creating the ultimate engine of the universe, the unified model that would maintain balance in the cosmos was the task to which Superforce Beth addressed herself. Indeed, if all went well, she would be "home" for the superforce.

Let us therefore examine the Force as it became manifest within cosmic Beth.

"Cosmic Beth is the secret of Hokhmah, the Force. She contains the mystery of *Nekudah B'Haihkalah*, the "Point of the Hall," for she represents Hesed (Mercy) of Hokhmah. The Light of Mercy is the hall or house for the Light of Wisdom (the Force). This is the ultimate in "blessing" (balance), a point illustrated by the Prophet Malahi in the verse, "I shall pour unto you a blessing, that there shall not be room enough to receive it."[23]

The light that "descends" from the Endless is not diffused
as it slices through the cosmos. From the beginning of its
journey to the end it is not deflected from its straight course
by any metaphysical fields of energy, or by any of the
curtains it passes through. Therefore, Beth pleaded that she
was suitable for the task of creation since she alone was not
affected by negative forces and influences. The Death Star
fleet, which was seeking to increase its dominion over the
cosmos, could not make any connection with Beth, the
Superforce, and thus could not use Beth as a source for
additional energy. Only at time of lack or deficiency does the
Death Star fleet find an opening by which to attack its
victim.[24]

Here for the first time, the *Zohar* provides us with a
glimpse into what constitutes "blessing." Any energy force,
any entity, or any man who is completely filled with energy
and who displays no lack, is considered blessed.

Examine an X-ray and we notice a black spot designating
the location of the problem. Why a black spot? To indicate
that the flow of energy is faltering and the Death Star fleet
has made an inroad. The lack of energy creates vulnerability
and thus an opportunity for the Dark Lord to make a surprise
attack. The removal of the black spot does not necessarily
restore the flow of energy. A state of blessing or completeness
is required, not the elimination of the Dark Lord.

Belief in the value and efficacy of blessing is attested to
in biblical narrations, such as those of Noah's blessing of
Shem and Japheth;[25] Isaac's blessing of Jacob and Esau;[26]
Jacob's blessing of his sons;[27] and of his grandsons, Ephraim
and Menasseh.[28] Blessing of children is usually given by the
father by "laying" the hands upon the head of the child and

pronouncing the verse (for a boy) "May the Lord make thee like Ephraim and Menasseh,"[29] followed by a priestly benediction[30] which contains a "threefold" arrangement, making explicit the intent of the ordained formula. The "laying on of hands" has long been known as a channel for the transference of energy.

"We have been taught: Whoever has attained the degree of Hesed (grace) is designated 'angel of the Lord of hosts,' as stated in the verse, 'For the priest's lips should keep knowledge, and they should seek the law at his mouth; for he is the angel of the Lord of hosts.'[31] Wherewith did the priest merit to be called 'angel of the Lord of hosts'? Said R. Judah: 'As the angel of the Lord of Hosts is a priest on high, so is the priest below an angel of the Lord of hosts.' Who is the celestial high priest? Angel Michael who issues from the celestial, cosmic force of Hesed."[32]

The priest was established as the chariot, the link, between the sfirah Hesed and the terrestrial realm. By virtue of the priest's embodiment of the force of Hesed, he was therefore considered the channel for blessing. The priest was the connection to the Superforce, the all embracing unified whole and therefore was endowed with the awesome power of the Force to bless mankind. The secret was the Light of Mercy, and that was the combination Beth presented to the Lord.

"And the Lord said to cosmic Beth, 'Most assuredly Beth, for your intrinsic characteristic is the perfect model by which the creative process and the world can achieve their Tikune.' This already has been hinted at by the Psalmist when he declares, 'For I have said, Hesed shall be built up forever.'[33]

The coded word 'shall be built up' also means understanding. The Lord established cosmic Beth as a criterion by which to discriminate between those forces or manifestations that are connected with the Force and those entities or manifestations which are linked to the Dark Lord. When humankind is drawn to the energies of imparting-restriction, cosmic Beth furnishes the force of blessing, as indicated in the verse,[34] 'And test me now herewith, said the Lord of hosts, if I will not open for you the windows of heaven, and pour out blessing that there not be room enough to receive it.'"[35]

In our discussion of time, it was noted that tomorrow is, of necessity, already included in yesterday. The principle of cause and effect, the seed already being included in the tree, and the double helix of DNA, all clearly in their separate ways demonstrate that the future depends on our ability to "see" it.

The future is here and now, but the illusionary one percent causes us to be blind to its presence. This one percent represents lack, incompleteness. Although illusionary, the one percent was essential to the cosmic process in that it imparted to us free will sufficient to relieve Bread of Shame. However, the illusion also caused an inability in us to "see" things as they are.

Beth's blessings fill the entire universal space of those individuals linked to Beth. The Superforce of cosmic Beth, implanted in and pervading the cosmos, allows those who are connected with the Superforce to not experience the illusionary defects within the creative process. This can be likened to an electric bulb, when circuitry exists, and one no longer observes the mechanism within the bulb. The moment that the light is switched on the poles and filament seem to disappear.

The truth of the matter is that the function of the opposing polarities in the filament are illusionary in as much as the light that supposedly appeared after turning on the switch was there in the first place. Light is everywhere, in the middle of a mountain, in the depths of the sea. Our illusionary perception of the light appears by our intervention, the physical effort of flipping the switch, which then disappears along with the physical components of the bulb. The physical effort involved is only one example among many which indicates that due to the original restriction which came about because of bread of shame, we humans were provided with an illusionary creative process that makes everything appear as if we are the creators of things around us.

The internal energy force of egocentricity, which is just another one of our illusions, was established for the express purpose of assisting us in achieving the objective of relieving bread of shame.[36] How? By merely connecting with the Superforce. The imparting (positive pole) and restriction (filament) of a light bulb is all the mechanism needed to restore the original all embracing unified light, removing it from its illusionary realm of darkness (incompleteness, lack, doubts, etc.). So, too, declares the Prophet Malahi, that by putting the Lord (the all embracing unified whole) to the test, by establishing the two energy-intelligences of imparting and restricting, "...if I will not open for you the windows of heaven, and pour out blessing, that there not be room enough to receive it."

The reader has undoubtedly heard, coming from an

electrician or others involved in repairing electrical appliances, the repeated declaration, "testing." Their concern is generally not whether the light will or will not come on, or whether there is electric current, but rather whether the mechanism (imparting-restriction intelligences) are functional.

So does the Prophet Malahi express this same concept of testing to determine whether there is lack or indecision in the Superforce. Blessing is constant and forever present. This is comparable to an electric current which is drawn into a home. The electricity is always there, but there are times when an internal connection with the electricity, such as the turning on of a light switch, has not been made. Where a connection has been established with the Superforce it is said to have been "built up forever" and that an unfailing "continuity" exists. Consequently, there is never "room enough to receive it," for it is constantly filled, with no room for more.

This is the "essence of change": defect, lack, deficiency, and incompleteness. Throughout history, the reputed leaders of civilization, up to and including the twentieth century, have always recommended change as the cure-all pill for better times ahead. We have been told that to understand our multifaceted structure of human existence, we must shift our perspective from the notion of static social structures to a perception of dynamic patterns of change. That transformation is thought to be an essential step in the development of civilization.

Proof of the necessity of transformation, we are told, is the fact that all civilizations have undergone cyclical processes of, genesis, growth, breakdown and disintegration. Arnold Toynbee, in his analysis of the genesis of civilization concluded that a transition from a static condition to one dynamic activity always existed in the developing process.[37] Toynbee, saw the basic patterns in the genesis of civilizations as a pattern of interaction which he called "challenge and response." In order to grow and respond to the challenges generated by the genesis process requires change, and "new" creative adjustments.

The kabbalist observes in this kind of reasoning the pervading force of the Dark Lord. Proof of the validity of any process does not lie in the evolution of the effect. It is no more or less significant than the corrupt conclusion that Jerusalem is the Holy City for the reason that the Holy Temple was located there. The kabbalist asks, "why was the temple there in the first place?" He therefore concludes that one must seek out the primal cause of things rather than get hung up in the effect.

Jerusalem is referred to as the Holy City for precisely the reason that it is referred to as "whole." It is the energy center of the universe, and therefore, as a natural consequence, the Holy Temple was located in Jerusalem. Any changes that occurred in Jerusalem were reflected in the effect, the Temple, and not in the holiness of the city of Jerusalem itself.

When change took place in Jerusalem, such as the destruction of the Temple, the presence of the Dark Lord and his Death Star fleet were in evidence. There is no city in the entire world where so much bloodshed has taken place. Nonetheless, the glamour, the importance, the mystique of Jerusalem continues uninterrupted despite the many nations that have temporarily superimposed their will over her cycle of history.

The kabbalist considers these changes part of the

illusionary reality which can only exist when inhuman activity severs the connection with the Superforce, and the Death Star fleet becomes the ruler of the terrestrial empire.

Why have so many nations considered Jerusalem to be the final grand prize in the quest for universal rule? The names, places or faces might have undergone illusionary changes, but the real participants followed a precise pattern: they were hungry for power. Their desire to receive remained an insatiable and unfulfilled desire. Lack is the key word, the illusionary force of the Dark Lord.

Jerusalem, the energy center of the world, is the terrestrial space station for the Superforce. This energy brought the convergence of all powerful empires to Jerusalem's doorstep. These nations represented an aspect of the Death Star fleet inasmuch as their primary concern was to connect with the Superforce in order to repair their defects and fulfill their wanton and covetous needs.

There was no cultural, evolutionary, or creative process involved in these "changing" situations. They followed the pattern of the Death Star fleet the prime concern of which is to instill the energy-intelligence of "desire to receive for oneself alone." The result of this pattern was constant and static uniformity, which ultimately caused the intruding forces to be severed from the Superforce and thus from Jerusalem.

The pattern described seems to fit our current situation very well. We are constantly subjected to theories concerning our evolutionary process in this new age. And yet, there is nothing new under the sun. As King Solomon, the wise, declared: "The thing that hath been, it is that which shall be;

and that which is done is that which shall be done: and there is no new thing under the sun".[38]

The Prophet Malahi stated it all so eloquently when he said that Blessing, the Superforce, is ever-present and all pervading, there isn't room enough to receive more.

Now we can understand the familiar phrase "when the novelty wears off." How often have we gone out to purchase an expensive suite of furniture and the moment it arrives, or shortly thereafter, we no longer have the same desire for it. What happened? The answer, states the *Zohar*, [39]is the lack of communication with cosmic Beth, the Superforce, the energy-intelligence of Blessing. When we are connected, meaning when human activity belongs in a frame of sharing-restriction, the negative energy of the Dark Lord does not prevail.

Doubt, uncertainty, lack of fulfillment, are the trademarks of the Death Star fleet which sometimes controls man, despite his illusionary, egocentric response that he simply "changed" his mind. However, when human activity becomes manifest with sharing and restriction, the Death Star fleet must retreat. The assault by positive energy-intelligence is too much for the Dark Lord to deal with. In Reality, there are no changes, no deficiencies, no doubts or illusions. When connected with the Superforce Beth, Man achieves a beautiful clarity of things. This is the true and encompassing energy-intelligence of cosmic Beth, the Superforce, the ultimate blessing.

What seems to emerge from our analysis of our mundane existence is that most people's lives are largely immersed in illusion, fear of want, unfulfilled dreams: in a word, change.

What, then, does reality consist of? Blessing. No change. This is the idea the Prophet Malahi describes when he declares "For I am the Lord, I change not; therefore you sons of Jacob are not consumed."[40]

How much time and effort is "consumed" by the unknowable. The measure of despair and frustration is incalculable. Are these necessary fixtures to mundane existence? The words of prophet Malahi are quite clear. So long as there exists a cosmic connection between ourselves with the Force (The Lord), there are no changes, since changes exist only in the world of illusion, the domain of the Dark Lord.

Let us now explore the Death Star fleet's inability to penetrate the security shield of the Superforce, Cosmic Beth. Where and how did frustration, defect, lack and despair become the hallmark of the Death Star fleet? How were they established within the intrinsic character of the Dark Lord, and what was the primal cause?

"The Dark Lord was sterile and had no capacity to yield the fruits of continuity."[41] Herein lies the mystery surrounding the energy-intelligence intrinsic in the character of the Dark Lord. Their essence consisted of and was bound up with the idea of the short circuit of quantum uncertainty as described by Heisenberg. Does this imply that uncertainty of quantum and the Death Star fleet are cut, so to speak, from the same cloth?

From the *Zohar* has emerged the unique quality of Superforce Beth. She was an instrument by which uncertainty, doubts, illusions would not become manifest so long as mankind could maintain the connection with the Superforce.

This appears to be in direct contradiction to Neils Bohr's interpretation of quantum paradoxes. Bohr concluded that the quantum reality reflects a basic limitation of the mind's ability to conceptualize "reality."

The trend in computer science points in the same direction. What the mind cannot achieve, the computer can accomplish. Who could fail to be awed by the ease with which computerized operations give amazing details of all known sciences?

This idea of uncertainty gained further momentum with Heisenberg's now famous discovery of the so-called "uncertainty principle." His finding played a crucial role in Bohr's interpretation of quantum theory. Heisenberg proved that nature conforms to the quantum theory's random description of subatomic behavior. Nature, he claimed, always draws a veil across her face whenever a scientist makes an attempt to obtain precise information.

The kabbalist never believed that the human mind must be chained to a precise set of reality concepts simply because of the inadequacy of language. Heisenberg produced his own language using sets of conceptual tools to describe reality and its counterpart, the physical illusionary reality. He believed that all physical reality, which includes subatomic particles, change at the whim of the human observer. And since the quantum reality implies that we must take virtually the whole universe into account when seeking the true cause of any physical event, we might as well say farewell to physics as it has been practiced for the past several hundred years.

Superforce Beth is in some ways similar to quantum mechanics, but with an added dimension of precise determinism which depends on whether one applies the restriction-imparting energy-intelligence of human activity or chooses to indulge in the desire to receive for oneself alone. Selfish activity creates a program of uncertainty in which even the most seemingly flawless plans become subject to quantum indecision. However, when the format of his program consists of the energy-intelligence of restriction-imparting, the individual can then access the Superforce Beth as the program for his or her daily existence. When this occurs, everything becomes improved, even beyond the best laid plans of the individual. The Superforce removes all the rough edges and replaces any doubts or uncertainty with Blessing.

Let us reach into the cosmic code of the universe, the Bible, for a deeper interpretation of the Superforce Beth within the cosmos. "R. Hiya then began to discourse on the text: 'When thou hast eaten and art satisfied, then thou shalt bless the Lord.'[42] Said he: 'Should a man then bless the Lord only after he has filled his belly? Nay, even if one eats but a morsel and "considers" (desires, meditates) it as a complete meal, this is referred to as eating to satisfaction: as it is written, Thou opens Thine hand and satisfiest the "desire" of every living thing.'[43] The verse does not state 'thou satisfiest with a substantial meal', so it is not the quality of food but the intention of it that 'satisfies'; therefore it is necessary that at all times when we eat we should bless the Lord, so as to provide joy to the cosmos."[44]

The literal reader of the Bible, the traditionalist, learns from scriptures that we are to thank the Lord for our daily bread. The verse, however, states very clearly that "when thou hast 'eaten' and art 'satisfied' then bless the Lord. As a fundamentalist, I find it hard-pressed to understand the verse any other way than is stated, namely, bless the Lord after we have eaten. Furthermore, although we have eaten, we still are not required to bless the Lord until we are satisfied which is a far cry from the traditional interpretation of the verse by all Judeo-Christian religions.

However, R. Hiya, in the *Zohar*, decodes for us this very complex and abstruse verse by hinting at another meaning for the word "satisfaction." We know all too well that for many a morsel of food may be satisfying and yet for others there is seldom enough food on the table. Therefore, R. Hiya concludes that the word for 'satisfaction' is completely bound up with the desire of the individual and not the amount that has been provided for by the Lord.

R. Hiya's interpretation makes it clear that the Psalmist paves the way in providing an insight into the world of reality by stating that satisfaction is not in the physical, illusionary realm of the actual food, its quantity or quality, but in the manifestation of blessing, Superforce Beth.

How does R. Hiya come to this conclusion? Because the Psalmist correlates the concept and idea of 'satisfaction' with the desire of the individual. In addition, for most of my readers, the idea of blessing the Lord does not sit well. Does the Lord need our blessing? The reverse might seem more appropriate.

What has emerged from this dilemma is the replacment of the word "Barukh" (blessing) with "Thank thee Lord." Corruptions of this nature are to be found throughout scriptures where the written word does not provide a satisfactory explanation. But as kabbalists, we know that the Bible represents the cosmic code of our universe and that the *Zohar* struggles successfully to decipher the code.

"The blessings that man blesses the Lord with are the metaphysical connections by which life is drawn from the wellspring of Life, Cosmic Binah to the Holy Name (Desire to Receive)[45] of the Lord, and to pour down from the supernal oil and from there to be drawn to the entire universe."[46]

What seems to emerge from the Zohar is a striking, if not daring, interpretation of what is known to most of religionists as "blessings." The word "blessing" simply represents another of the Biblical codes, and in this particular case the *Zohar* states that blessing is the connection with Superforce Beth.

When "desire" or "intent" is accessed to the software of restriction-sharing, the individual is simultaneously connected with Superforce Beth, where a morsel of food, or whatever, represents complete satisfaction. One feels no hunger pains if one is connected with Beth's Superforce, even if he has eaten only a morsel, and nor will he feel indigestion because of overeating. Superforce Beth leaves no room for lack, defeat, deficiency, or even uncertainty. Beth leaves nothing to chance.She leaves no stones unturned. Never does she find it necessary to change her plans. Everything is right from the outset.

At the same time, we as individuals have been provided with the free will to either experience the hell of uncertainty, becoming an associate of the Dark Lord and his Death Star fleet, or to connect with the Superforce of the Lord.

Whether we *Homo sapiens* concern ourselves with the physical pleasures of life or the more serious ventures that deal with family, livelihood, or life itself, the uncertainty principle shall always be an intrinsic and integral part of our existence. We shall commonly be plagued by a desire to turn the clock back, to undo that which we have created, to stop the clock if we could. This is what the *Zohar* alludes to when it states, "The Dark Lord was 'sterile' and had no capacity to yield the fruits of continuity."

Therefore, the Dark Lord is sterile inasmuch as the desire to receive for oneself alone does not contain an energy-intelligence of continuity. When desire turns into an energy-intelligence of the "desire to receive for oneself alone" it causes an abrupt halt to the flow of the Light of the Lord, the Force.

The desire to receive for oneself alone, represented by the negative pole of an electric bulb, is a classic example of the Dark Lord in action. The filament represents the energy-intelligence of restriction. When the filament of the bulb becomes non-functional we observe a black spot around the area where short-circuit became manifest. Observe further that for a split second after the filament 'pops,' one can still observe the presence of electric current going through the bulb. This is because the electric current is ever present, as is the remaining functional negative energy-intelligence of the negative pole. However, since there is no continuity, due to connection being severed between the Superforce Beth and the physical bulb, the Dark Lord can now penetrate the bulb's security shield. The Death Star fleet's presence becomes observable by the dark spot around the bulb.

Consequently, the bulb ceases to give the appearance of providing light. Discontinuity, the intrinsic characteristic of the Dark Lord, has set in, taking over the bulb's mini-universe. The broken thread, interruption, uncertainty, these are the trademarks of the Death Star fleet. Hence the light must cease.

Another example that we might make use of to further our understanding of the Dark Lord and what constitutes severance from Superforce Beth, is turning on or off a television or radio. Despite our desire and intent the sound of the radio or the television picture still continues for a few seconds after we have turned the knob or pressed the button to the off position. The on position represents the activation of the energy-intelligence of restriction-imparting. When the knob is turned off, the aspect of restriction-imparting ceases to be operational. However, the broadcasting station is not affected in the least by the knob being turned to an off position. So it is with Superforce Beth.

The knob at the off position indicates severance from the Superforce. It also signals the opportunity for the Death Star to invade and nourish from the flow of the Force. However, because of the Dark Lord's sterility and inability to maintain continuity, the Force ceases to become observable within our limited frame of reference — this despite its constant presence on the airwaves and also within millions of other televisions and radios.

Now uncertainty enters the scene of the present. At this moment, the conclusion of the program, or whatever was to follow on the broadcasting station, remains uncertain. The viewer could only guess what the conclusion or following program is going to be about. Moreover, the viewer's uncertainty does not dictate uncertainty for others. There exists for the viewer a temporary "illusion" that broadcasting has ceased, inasmuch as he is not a kabbalist and therefore cannot view or perceive the ongoing broadcast on a radio or television set where the connection with the Superforce still continues.

Were the viewer capable of maintaining a link with Superforce Beth, the uncertainty that becomes manifested within most of us would not exist. The possibility to view the ongoing program schedule would be a distinct reality. Unfortunately, most of humankind does not maintain a constant energy-intelligence of restriction-imparting and consequently their connection with the Superforce is severed.

Those of us who maintain a constant link with Superforce Beth establish a connection with all that is being broadcast throughout the entire universe. The bond with Superforce Beth is the assurance that the Dark Lord with his Death Star fleet cannot penetrate the security shield established by the self-administered energy-intelligence of restriction-imparting. The illusionary idea of uncertainty, lack, defect or discontinuity has no place in the world of reality. The realm of imperfection is the exclusive domain of scientists and others who might like to join the uncertainty club.

This is precisely the concept presented by the *Zohar*. "R. Shimon spoke on the verse: 'And thou O Lord, be not far from me; O my strength, haste thou to help me.'[47] Said he (R. Shimon): The two invocations 'thou' and 'Lord' represent Malkhuth and Tifereth respectively, or the two worlds, one of illusion (Malkhuth) and reality (Tifereth). The Psalmist prayed that they become united and not separate from each other. For when the one separates from the other, all light is darkened and removed from the world. Our universe receives its nourishment, positive energy from Malkhuth, but when Malkhuth, which is the lower light, does not receive its strength from Tifereth, she has nothing to offer this universe.

For this reason, indeed, was the Temple destroyed in the time of Jeremiah; humankind caused a severance in the link between Tifereth and Malkhuth."[48] The awesome power of Superforce Beth had been abandoned by human negative activity.

What seems to emerge from the preceding *Zohar* is the potential dual activity that appears to be present in all energy-intelligent activity. This is precisely the mystery that is generated within the subatomic world of particles which drives physicists insane. Sometimes these particles combine, change into one another and then suddenly fall apart.

The *Zohar* drives home the point that if negative human activity prevails, then an illusionary severance between energy (Tifereth) and matter (Malkhuth) seems to take place. The reason behind this cosmic activity — which becomes manifest at all levels, from the cosmos down to the terrestrial realm of subatomic activity — is that humankind has severed the cosmic bond with Superforce Beth resulting in a takeover by the Death Star fleet. Thus the Dark Lord sets in motion the illusionary disintegration of matter, the uncertainty, the process of discontinuity.

Let us, nevertheless, not forget that a parallel universe exists for that segment of humankind, who maintain their connection with Superforce Beth and is alive and well. Continuity, fulfillment, the joy of certainty never cease.

The *Zohar* provides an amusing picture of our universe, an image that is intuitively pleasing and that hints at an ultimate simplicity. In addition to providing an amazing description of our environment, R. Shimon demonstrates and brings home the idea of two parallel universes bound up and linked to Superforce Beth when he discusses the ten martyrs.

"O Lord, how did your children, the foundation of the universe, upon whom the world depended, and I became crowned through their good deeds, suffer such a degrading death at the hands of the Dark Lord. How were their spirits so debased? Despite the fact that when the ten sages were led to their inhuman deaths and their holy bodies were "substituted" with bodies of the Death Star fleet, nevertheless, your Holy Name was desecrated. Those who witnessed the slaying were under the impression that the holy bodies of these sages were being tormented."[49]

The sages were experiencing the very peculiar sensation of having "two" bodies, the illusionary body which belonged to the realm of the Dark Lord, the painful physical one, and the other, the holy body, linked up to Superforce Beth. Strange as this phenomena might sound to many readers of this book, may I state that the *Zohar* is replete with many similar illustrations of two parallel universes, the world of reality and the realm of the illusion.

Prior to the advent of the twentieth century scientific revolution, illusion meant an incorrect perception of external stimuli. Familiar examples are those that occur in mirages, and also when a tailor's dummy is mistaken for a living person, or when stationary lights seem to move in an advertising display, or even when a straight spoon appears to bend when submerged in a glass of water.

Today, however, with uncertainty established as an integral component of perception, the foregoing ideas do not necessarily lead to false beliefs or conclusions. Illusion no longer seems to arise from or through distorted transmission of external stimuli. What is perceived by the individual may in essence be considered reality, and what most of us perceive as reality may in fact be connected to the false impression of the illusionary world.

In a sense, it is meaningless to argue which view is correct, since, as quantum physics has taught us, nature's elemental properties defy objective evaluation. The immediate effect of uncertainty is that there is a "real" domain beyond, only that man with his present limitations is not capable of entering that domain. Some will, therefore, conclude that the failure of the physical law of cause and effect provides the solution concerning the problem of freedom of will. On the other hand, the atheist will now have found justification for his contention that chance rules the universe.

The *Zohar* and Superforce Beth seem to be the only way out of this dilemma. Cosmic Beth is the link to certainty, the realm beyond the clutches of the Dark Lord and all that he portrays and represents. The implications and benefits of the Superforce are profound and too numerous to even begin to conceptualize what effect the new realm of reality might have on the overall mental and physical well being of all of us. After all, how can we begin to entertain a treatment of any kind if our diagnosis is based in uncertainty.

The Superforce connects us with the idea of holistic medicine which takes into account all aspects of a patient's life in the final diagnosis and treatment. The mind, our attitude, is an essential ingredient to the improvement of our well being. Superforce is the link to completeness.

Another fine example of the way the Dark Lord can manipulate our sense of reality concerns the Zoharic description of the Biblical narration surrounding the Golden Calf image made by Aaron at the behest of the Israelites and venerated near Mt. Sinai.[50] Thereupon the Lord told Moses of the apostasy of the Israelites, whom he proposed to destroy. Carrying the Tablets of the Covenant down from Mt. Sinai, Moses saw the people dancing around the Golden Calf. In great anger, Moses smashed the Tablets, melted down the image of the calf, pulverized the precious metal and scattered the powdered gold over the available source of water, thus making the people drink it.

The *Zohar* departs from the original narration and comes to another conclusion, namely, that the tablets were not shattered.

Said R. Akiba to his students, "Do not compare pure marble to other stone which contains energy-intelligences of life and death. We know this from the scriptures, 'A wise man's heart is at his right hand, but a fool's heart at his left.'[51] The original Tablets were made from pure marble material and therefore no separation or discontinuity was present. It was only an illusion to consider the Tablets as having been broken."[52]

The idea that there exists two separate and distinct realities is a concept very close to home for the magician. Sawing a woman in half with a laser beam is a specific example of the modern sophistication of the illusionary art of magic. Harry Houdini would have had a field day with Kabbalah. In fact, legend has it that he was acquainted with Kabbalah.

The magical phenomenon of an entire aircraft vanishing before the very eyes of a massive sea of people is an accomplished fact. What magicians accomplish is to reawaken the realm of reality that lies dormant in all of us. As children, we were fascinated by a leaf turning colors. It seemed to us that we were witnessing a miracle until we were taught that when the leaf loses chlorophyll it changes colors and dies. We are taught not to be fascinated by such things.

The Bible seems to make it perfectly clear that when Moses descended from Mt. Sinai, "And he cast the Tablets out of his hands, and broke them he shattered the Tablets beneath the mount."[53] There seems to be an apparent contradiction between the *Zohar's*[54] interpretation of the "shattering" of the Tablets and that of the Bible itself.

Once again, the *Zohar* brings to our attention the two realities that became established when Adam sinned. The Tree of Life represented the true reality whereas the Tree of Knowledge brought into existence the world of illusion. When Adam became severed from Superforce Beth, the reality realm became concealed and a veil of illusion made its appearance. Thus, was born the world of uncertainty.

In essence, the Tablets were never shattered. These were to be later placed in the ark. When the High Priest accessed to the Tablets, he connected with and drew awesome power from the cosmos. For the sinners of the Golden Calf, the veil of illusion, the energy-intelligence of uncertainty became their realm of reality.

Another example of illusionary existence is the mistaken belief that the Holy Temple in Jerusalem was set afire by the Romans and destroyed. Not so, claims the *Zohar*. If ever the intelligent energy of illusion became manifested in totality, it is the *Zohar's* contention that this occurred regarding the destruction of the Holy Temple.

The historical account of Roman conquest of the Holy Land and the subsequent destruction of the Temple and the carrying off into slavery of over 100,000 Jews, the slaughter of hundreds of thousands more remains to this day a vivid testimonial of a Temple no more.

To accept this notion — when anyone visiting the Temple Mount cannot visually observe a Temple — is something that every human being will be hard-pressed to accept. However, with uncertainty becoming an integral part of our understanding of things around us, one cannot disprove the contention of the *Zohar*. According to the *Zohar* the essence of the temple is still there, only the illusion was destroyed.

When physicists realized that the concept of the perfect all-knowing, all-embracing unified whole seems to have no support in nature, classical physics came to an abrupt halt. It is precisely for this reason that scientists today can no longer initiate grants and fellowships for their studies in the physical sciences, for, indeed, like the alchemists of old, they have become metaphysicians!

Despite their conclusions concerning the quantum theory — that everything in our observable universe is uncertain — scientists still pursue a theory of grand unification. Why? Because something tells them that beyond quantum there exists a deterministic universe, a true metaphysical reality.

This uncertainty relationship applies to a single measurement as well as a statistical average. To achieve the realm of deterministic reality, one must raise one's level of consciousness. This requires the connection with Superforce Beth, which transcends the illusionary frame of reference.

Quantum discoveries did not, as physicists believe, prove that the universe is indeterminate. Quantum merely indicates that our conscious mind cannot grasp all of reality at once. A new vision of reality is now necessary. The *Zohar* contends that the answer to this and all physical dilemmas lies in the transcendence of the conscious mind, which itself is of the illusion. There is no randomness, once our consciousness has been raised. This, unfortunately, is not the path science has chosen.

"Over those stones of the former foundations other nations could prevail, inasmuch as they lacked a higher consciousness of energy intelligence... Heaven forbid to think for a moment that other nations ruled over the foundations of Zion and Jerusalem. They did not torch them, nor were they burnt. They became concealed by the Lord and there wasn't lost even one stone. However, when the Light of reality returns, the only people to observe it will be those whose eyes have been raised to a higher consciousness. For the others, the illusion will reign."[55]

This is precisely the idea Prophet Malahi presents when he declares, "You shall return and discern between the righteous and the wicked, between him that serveth the Lord and him that serveth Him not."[56]

In the absence of a better translation, I have accepted the conventional version of this profound and penetrating verse. However, make no mistake that the idea of serving the Lord is to be understood within a frame of connection. When a link between ourselves and Superforce Beth has been established, there is certainty. The idea of uncertainty is initiated solely by the "desire to receive for oneself alone."

"The Creator did not reveal the Light of Blessing in order to bring about the perfection and correction of the world. Instead, Blessing serves only as a good beginning, which is essential in bringing about the final and complete correction."[57]

Questions about the nature of reality can be subtle indeed. It can be extraordinarily difficult to conclude just what is real and what is part of the illusion. The truths contained in the *Zohar* provide for the possibility that we will one day make sense out of our existence. All that is required is connection to Superforce Beth.

This was the blessing cosmic Beth could provide for all mankind. The connection was indeterminate. However, Beth was a good starting point for achieving Blessing.

Draw the "blessing" of Superforce Beth more into our terrestrial realm and observe the consequence when one has not made the cosmic connection. The situation I am addressing is the physics society. The reader might mistakenly assume that I have singled out the physics community for criticism. Nothing could be further from the truth — it is just that any negative approach simply hasn't turned the light on.

My intention is to bring home the importance of Superforce Beth as an essential ingredient in the lexicon of life's existence, which embraces all facets of our physical reality. Many physicists, along with a large percentage of politicians, have failed dismally in their search for the cure to the ills of society.

Consider the latest research by physicist Frank Avignone, professor of physics at the university of South Carolina, who has spent six years of his life and $1,300,000 of government money — peanuts in this day and age — only to arrive at still more uncertainty. This is a sorry state of affairs, especially in view of the fact that "With fame goes money" has become a scientific slogan of the day.

The record of science is indeed disappointing. Recently, the Reagan administration has given the go-ahead to build the ultimate atom smasher at a cost of at least $4.5 billion. The objective? To recreate a veritable blast from the past, the condition which they think may have existed one thousandth of a trillionth of a second *after* the Big Bang.

Will this, like other scientific ego trips, prove to be just another exercise in futility? Ultimately, the greed of scientists shall bring about their own demise. Uncertainty, the world of physical reality, leads down a one-way street of illusion. No atom smasher, no matter how much it costs or how well it is designed, will ever move us out of the realm of uncertainty.

Contrarily, the path to certainty is a one-way ticket to Superforce Beth. All other roads lead to frustration, lack, greed and negativity, the Tree of Knowledge. The Superforce Beth is the high-road to "Blessing."

22

The Letter Aleph

It is not your part to finish the task;
yet neither are you free to desist from it.

— Rabbi Tarfon, "Ethics of the Fathers"

Cosmic Beth, with the energy-intelligence of "blessing," represented the ideal channel for the network of universal communications. Only she could prevent humanity from becoming eternally disconnected from the Force. Now that Beth was established as the creative channel, humanity would never have to succumb to total robotic consciousness and the Death Star fleet would be prevented from dominating the universe by removing all vestiges of free will from the human psyche.

With the matter of universal creation and stability well in hand, cosmic Aleph had no cause to come forward to enter a plea to become a suitable channel for the creation. Nor did she have that desire, for she understood and was satisfied with her role in the cosmic scheme. She was to be a silent partner in the realm of thought-communication. It would be her function to link the other letter-energies, bridging the illusion of space between them.

From the onset, the Lord recognized the purpose for each letter's participation in the creative process. The letters, whether they would be chosen as the channel for the creative process or not, were ultimately a part of the celestial mechanism for communication with the supreme energy of cosmic intelligence. Obviously, then, the Lord was aware of Aleph's actual place in the universal plan. And yet still He saw fit to question Aleph as to why she did not come forward.[1] Before we examine that dialogue, let us delve briefly into other matters of related interest.

Here is the way that King David described the Supreme Intelligence:
"Bless the Lord, O my soul. O Lord, my Lord, thou art very great; thou art very great, thou art clothed with honor and majesty. Who coverest thyself with light as with a garment: who stretches out the heavens like a curtain: who layeth the beams of his chambers in the waters: who maketh the clouds his chariot: who walketh upon the wings of the wind: who maketh the winds his messengers; the flames of fire his ministers."
"...who laid the foundations of the earth, that it should not be removed forever. Thou

coverest it with the deep as with a garment. The waters stand above the mountains."

"At thy rebuke they fled; at the voice of thy thunder they hasted away."

"They go up by the mountains; they go down by the valleys unto the place which thou hast founded for them."

"Thou hast set a bound that they may not pass over; that they turn not again to cover the earth."

"He sendeth the springs into the valleys, which run among the hills....He appointed the moon for seasons; the sun knoweth his going down. Thou makest darkness and it is night.... Thou sendest forth thy spirit, they are created and thou renewest the face of the earth."[2]

Kabbalists say that the thinking process converts knowledge to energy. A verse in Genesis alludes to the concept of the intimacy between knowledge and energy when it states, "And Adam knew Eve his wife; and she conceived and bore Cain."[3] In this verse we find the dynamic interplay between 'knowing' and the energy of the sexual union of man and woman. The biblical connotation of *knowing* and sexual intercourse are, of course, inextricably bound up with each other.

Many people communicate with the Force on a daily basis through prayer, meditation, or with other mental activity. Yet despite the fact that it is an integral aspect in the majority of human lives, the Force is scientifically undetectable. Nor can the soul, that part of the Force which we carry around inside us, be identified by current scientific means. Does this in any way imply that the Force does not exist? Of course not. It means only that the scientific method is an inadequate means of detecting its existence. In nature we find an infinite number of indications that a formative intelligence shaped and structured everything in its proper order.

The opinion that the scientific method is inadequate is no longer adhered to only by kabbalists. This, along with the idea that verbal descriptions suffer from the deficiency of language, has now been commonly accepted also by quantum physicists. Both the kabbalist and the physicist have arrived at the conclusion that reality transcends our common language.

"The problems of language here are really serious. We wish to speak in some way about the structure of the atoms.... But we cannot speak about atoms in ordinary language." So said the quantum physicist, Werner Heisenberg, discoverer of the Uncertainty Principle.[4]

Both the kabbalist and the physicist are attempting to identify the connection between thought and reality, but until recently only the kabbalist has been aware that to do so requires the transcendence of the limits of our sensory thought processes. The problem the scientists encounter is the lack of a common and universal language that might characterize the essential, internal (some say indescribable) nature of all things.

"Anyone not making use of the Torah (the cosmic code of the universe) and who does not apply or put to use his or her knowledge, is removed from the Lord and distant from Him. The result of which is that the *Shekhinah* (the embodiment of revelation) does not dwell upon him. And those angels (housing the super-intelligence) are removed from him.

"Woe unto him, for the upper and lower dimensions of energy-intelligence abandon him and he no longer participates in the living interplay of things."[5]

Shekhinah! Here we find in a single word a description of mankind's key to the universal energy-intelligence. Shekhinah is the confluence of all potential energy and the point at which the Light is revealed. Man's responsibility lies in whether or not to patch into this vast, profound energy-intelligence that is the basis for all physical revelation.

Although the macro and microworlds seem from our limited perspective in this world of illusion to be two distinct and separate entities, there is no reason why they must remain so. To unite and combine reality with illusion, the metaphysical and the physical, requires the cosmic code of the Torah as it is channeled through the Aleph Beth. In addition, there is the need for our conscious participation in the cosmic process.

Kavannot (direction), the conscious direction of our awareness through meditation, is an integral aspect of the cosmic connection. Failure to utilize *kavannot* is like having a full telephone communications system but never using it. It is strange indeed that until recently scientists obstinately insisted on keeping kavannot (consciousness) out of any and all discussions of the physical world. Is it not our consciousness through which we perceive the world around us, formulate opinions, and make observations — even those of a scientific nature? Does it not seem ludicrous, then, that for almost four centuries science failed to consider, much less grasp, the obvious interaction between the worlds of mind and matter?

Quantum Theory verifies several kabbalistic tenets by introducing consciousness into the scientific lexicon, but at the same time it suggests a new potential danger. Quantum findings seem to indicate that random chance, rather than a supreme motivating influence, prevails as the motivating principle at work in the universe. From the quantum perspective there seems to be only one universal law and that is the law of averages. Thus, Heisenberg's Uncertainty Principle might be seen as establishing a new and dangerous perspective on the aspect of free will. The danger is that total, unbridled free will might be seen as absolving man of all responsibility for his actions. Whereas Kabbalah attributes life to a single supreme source, Quantum perceives only randomness. With random chance as the motivating influence of the cosmos, anything might be likely to happen, violence, death, war and destruction, but the finger of blame could point to no one. Who, after all, could possibly be held accountable if there is no one or nothing to be accountable to?

The Bible foresaw the inherent danger of this free-wheeling attitude and took steps to reconcile the seeming dichotomy between free will and determinism. By deciphering the cosmic code, with the help of the *Zohar*, kabbalists arrived at an understanding of the coexistence of these two aspects within the universal scheme.

The kabbalistic world view might be likened to quantum without the randomness.[6] Both the kabbalist and the quantum physicist agree that everything in the universe is interrelated. The only intrinsic difference between them seems to be that the physicist has not yet made the perceptual leap which will allow him to see beyond the disorderly arrangements which seem to be taking place in the tiny window through which he views the physical world.

As we mentioned in *Kabbalah for the Layman*,[7] the universe never has and never will abide in a state of chaos. Disorder, holocaust, war and suffering are all limited in their scope, and all are the result of human activity. The *Tsimtsum*, the great restriction that initiated the physical universe, brought forth one vital feature of enduring value, the possibility of earning the Light's blessing by removing Bread of Shame. This seemingly chaotic physical universe, then, from the kabbalistic perspective, is an illusion that we selected for the purpose of providing ourselves with free will and the opportunity for restriction.[8]

According to the principle of restriction, the eternal order of the cosmos, along with its all-embracing intelligence, must conceal itself so as to make it appear as if mankind, through his choice of activity, selects and determines the appropriate degree of cosmic order. However, this illusion should not be mistaken with the idea that man is the ongoing, day-to-day determiner of universal activity. For the human being, free will is directed toward and limited by the opportunities that arise from time to time which allow him to exercise restriction.

Kabbalah teaches that the physical universe and the laws that govern it are, by the infinite standard, illusionary. By achieving an altered state of consciousness, one can gain entrance to the higher all-knowing, all-embracing cosmic intelligence in which linear time and space are transcended and the true, infinite reality can be perceived. By tapping this profound universal energy-intelligence one becomes impervious to the randomly chosen programs which are the lot of those who fail to exercise voluntary restriction.

The kabbalistic conclusion on the matter of free will is

that each individual's program or personal life-path is chosen
from an infinite selection of "software," but that free will
exists only to the extent that each of us is allowed to choose
our own program. Once chosen, all of the subsequent
parameters are predetermined. When one puts a coin in a
computer arcade game, for instance, he or she cannot
suddenly decide to play another game on that same machine.
Another analogy might be that of throwing a stone. Once you
let it go you have no more say in the matter. Free will has
been instantly replaced by the laws of cause and effect.

The basic patterns of life were structured from beginning
to end by the Force at the inception of the universe. Thus,
the extent of our free will lies solely in whether to restrict
and thus claim the right to choose between an infinite number
of programs, or to succumb to desire to receive for oneself
alone and allow ourselves to be ruled by iron hand of
determinism.

With all this behind us, let us now return to the question
raised at the beginning of this chapter. Each letter, including
cosmic Aleph, was necessary for the ultimate connection with,
and the tapping of, cosmic intelligence. Why then did the
Lord have tocall upon Aleph to come forward?

Control over the process of universal formation was
established by cosmic Beth. It was because of her *berakhah*
(blessing) intelligence over the creative process that life on
earth inherited such a favorable setting for its development.
The cosmic intelligence operating outside the material realm,
guided by the *berakhah* intelligence, would be sufficient for
maintaining the proper balance and symmetry between the
positive and negative polarities, good and evil. This
cosmological phenomenon, an essential element of universal

balance, was earth's guarantee that the Death Star fleet would never assume dominion over this vast solar empire.

Cosmic Aleph is the intrinsic thought-intelligence of 'air' which made possible and established the "steady state" framework of our universe.[9] Nothing really changes. The original Big Bang was only the most intense of infinite trillions of miniature big bangs which were to follow — all of which are returned to a unified steady state of activity by cosmic Aleph. Whether we are speaking of explosions involving high or low density matter, or no-density metaphysical phenomena, the basic underlying principle is the same. In all cases, the unifying steady state factor is Aleph.

Let us briefly examine the process of picking up a pebble and tossing it into the sea. Because the process first takes place in the mind of the person who is going to throw the pebble, the thrower's desire must be included as an integral part of the process. The outcome is determined in the mind of the thrower *before* he or she tosses the pebble. The result, with a few minor variations, is predetermined, established in the mind and carried out by the laws of cause and effect. The stone, itself, plays a fairly insignificant role in the process. What, then, causes the splash and subsequent ripples? The kabbalist says the mind.

As for the circles of waves around the pebble when it strikes the water, we might expect the largest ripple to occur at impact because of the water's resistance to the pebble's violent intrusion into its domain. Yet it is farther away from the initial invasion that we encounter the largest waves. This phenomenon is carefully explained in my book, *Kabbalah for the Layman*. The larger outer waves reveal the thought-intelligence of the thrower. The thought-intelligence at its starting point (when the individual decided to throw the rock) carries with it a great deal more energy than those stages subsequent to the initial thought.

A similar situation exists relative to the interaction of forces connected with the making of a bomb. The bomb explodes first in the mind of its inventor who then proceeds to work on ideas as to how that explosion might be produced on a physical level. It then progresses through a cycle of thought-energy-intelligences within the minds of those who are producing and developing it, gaining power as it nears completion. Finally, possibly years later, when the bomb is detonated, the explosion (restriction) reveals the thought-energy-intelligence that existed first in the inventor's mind.

Before detonation, the bomb is in a potential steady state of thought-intelligence. It is only when the bomb strikes a target that the thought-intelligence is revealed on the corporeal level. At all levels of interaction between thought-energy and the vessel (the bomb), the same dynamic "big bang" interplay recurs, the only significant difference being in the nature of the materials, the density of matter and temperatures. Whether we are discussing the interaction between a pebble and water, an electrical current meeting up with the filament, or what goes on inside a nuclear reactor — all are determined according to the same fundamental principles.

A growing tree undergoes the process of restriction at each stage of its development. Before the trunk of a tree appears, the expanding root encounters restriction, which in turn permits further growth. This process repeats continually from the moment of planting until the final fruition. Indeed, expansion continues even after that. The seed of the new fruit undergoes another big bang when it falls to the ground or a planter inserts it into mother earth. Similarly, the universe in its expansion from the original Big Bang has encountered many times the thought-intelligence of restriction, the impact-point of which serves as a target for the next stage of universal evolution. That this universal process is uniform and in many ways predictable is a result of the energy-intelligence of Aleph.

Where is the drive for sustained activity coming from? Why, for instance, do parents desire children when they know very well the pain and heartache that will result from this activity? The answer lies in the original thought of creation which was the Lord's desire to share.[10] This on-going activity within the universe manifests itself at all levels of existence. Consequently, the basic building blocks of both animate and inanimate, thinking and non-thinking entities, are the same kinds of atoms. What is it, then, that distinguishes one from the other? The usual answer to this question has to do with the different arrangements of the atoms, but the kabbalist questions why should these different arrangements exist and what is the cause for their dissimilarity?

The difference lies in the levels of intensity of the desire to receive.[11] The greater is the desire, the greater the necessity for restriction. Resistance and the impact that develops between a negative thought-intelligence and its rejection manifests as a miniature big bang, the size and impact of which depends on the degree of desire. This particular function, throughout this and all other universes, is expressed by cosmic Aleph. The revelation of all steady state universes reveals Aleph's unique role in the cosmic scheme.

Obviously, cosmic Aleph fills a crucial need in the creative process. Why, then, did she fail to make manifest her energy-intelligence as had those before her? Why, also, did the Lord, when addressing Aleph, repeat her name twice?

Aleph's role as an extraterrestrial link with the Force is very distinct from that of her colleagues. Their respective channels served as access to the Force only when the initiative came from the vessels, the letter-energies themselves. Cosmic Aleph, however, could not initiate or make manifest *Myin Nukvin* (the vessel's energy-intelligence of desire to receive). Aleph's energy is derived solely from the Force.

This unique characteristic, intrinsic in cosmic Aleph, was revealed by the *Zohar*'s[12] interpretation of the verse in Prophet Amos, "The virgin of Israel (Shekhinah) is fallen; she shall no more rise."[13] The *Zohar* declares that the Shekhinah cannot rise from exile through her own effort. She shall be redeemed, however, only by the Lord Himself.

According to the *Zohar*,[14] the Shekhinah will undergo two periods of redemption. "See now. In all the other exiles of Israel a term was set, at the end of which Israel returned to the Lord and the Virgin of Israel came back to her place. But this last and present exile is not so, for she shall not return as on previous occasions. The verse in Amos indicates this also when it says, 'The virgin of Israel is fallen, she shall rise no more.' Note that it is not written, 'I shall not raise her any more.'

The *Zohar* describes a king who was wroth with his queen and banished her from his palace for a very long time, but then he could no longer bear her absence. Said the king, "This time is not like the other times when she came back to

me. This time I shall go with all my followers to find her."
When he came to her he found her lying in the dust. Seeing
her thus humiliated and yearning once more for her, the king
took her by the hand, raised her up, and brought her to his
palace and swore to her that he would never part from her
again.

So it is written: 'In that day I will raise up the tabernacle
of David that is fallen.'[15] The tabernacle of David being
identical with the virgin of Israel."

Whether during the illusionary period of 6,000 years
when mankind makes his effort at correction, or in the period
of the final emendation, cosmic Aleph will never initiate the
Myin Nukvin. When the other letters express the *Myin Nukvin*,
the proper thought-energy-intelligence of the vessel, or at the
time of the final correction, cosmic Aleph will act only as the
channel for the Force of the Lord to return *Myin Duhrin* to
the Infinite circular condition from which it first emerged.

Therefore, cosmic Aleph did not enter her plea to be the
channel for creation. Yet the Lord called her name twice,
"Aleph. Aleph..." Once for the purpose of transmitting
through Aleph the-Force, when human positive activity
prevailed, and again to establish the channel for the final
redemption. Having done this He told her, "You, Aleph, shall
be considered the Head of all the letters, for you represent
the upper three sfirot. The great unifying energy force, the
Head, will be revealed only through you."[16]

The energy infused within Beth embraces the force of
Genesis I, the Light of Mercy, which includes only the seven
lower bottled-up energies (sfirot) which govern this, the
World of Action. Consequently, the biblical code presented in
Genesis I is limited to the seven days of physical creation.

Beth is devoid of the Light Force of the "Head" or "First Three" sfirot, Keter, Hokhmah and Binah. Hers is the domain of the created illusion. It is Aleph who provides the vital link with the true, Infinite reality, the first three sfirot, also known as the Light of Wisdom.

Beth's Light of Mercy is not dependent upon man's activity. When man expresses and makes manifest negative thought-energy-intelligence, the power of cosmic Beth does not change. Beth maintains the Light but has no power to alter Its course or dimension. Like a thrown pebble, Beth's Light of Mercy, is no longer governed by the initiating factor. Having left the source it is now controlled by the laws of cause and effect. The *Mohin* (the Force of the Head), on the other hand, which is channelled by cosmic Aleph, depends entirely upon human activity. If man is evil, the *Mohin* of Aleph is rescinded. When, however, positive human thought activity prevails in the universe, then the grand unification force of the Lord is established by Aleph. Complete and eternal unification will take place at the time of the final emendation and correction. This, too, will manifest with the aid of the "silent partner," cosmic Aleph.

Appendices

APPENDICE I

THE LETTER KAF

לא) בההיא שעתא, נחתא מן קדמוהי את כ מעל כורסיה, יקריה,
ח אזדעזעת ואמרה קמיה: רבון עלמא, ניחא קמך למברי בי עלמא, דאנא
כבודך. וכד נחתת כ מעל כורסיה יקריה, אזדעזעו ו מאתן אלף עלמין
ואזדעזע כרסייא, וכלהו עלמין אזדעזעו למנפל. אמר לה קב"ה: כ"ף, כ"ף, מה
את עביד הכא, דלא אברי בך עלמא, תוב לאתרך, דהא בך כליה, ש כלה ונחרצה
אשתמע, תוב לכרסייך והוי תמן. בההיא שעתא נפקת מקמיה ותבת לדוכתה.

APPENDICE II

THE LETTER YOOD

לב) עאלת את י, אמרה קמיה: רבון עלמא, ניחא קמך למברי בי
עלמא, דאנא שירותא דשמא קדישא, ויאות לך למברי בי עלמא. אמר לה: די
לך דאנת חקיק בי, ואנת רשים בי, וכל רעותא דילי בך, סליק, לית אנת יאות
לאתעקרא מן שמי.

APPENDICE III

THE LETTERS TET AND HET

לג) עאלת את א) ט ה) אמרה קמיה: רבון עלמא, ניחא קמך למברי בי
עלמא, דאנת, בי אתקריאת טוב וישר. אמר לה: לא אברי בך עלמא, דהא
טובך סתים בגווך · וצפון בגווך, ההה״ד, ב) מה רב טובך אשר צפנת ליראך,
הואיל וגניז בגווך, לית ביה חולקא לעלמא דא, דאנא בעי למברי, אלא בעלמא
דאתי. ותו, דעל דטובך גניז בגווך, יטבעון תרעי דהיכלא. ההה״ד, ג) טבעו בארץ
שעריה. ותו ד) ד ה ה) לקבלך, וכד תתחברון כחדא, הא ה) ח״ט, ועל דא אתוון
אלין ו) לא רשימין בשבטין קדישין, מיד נפקת מקמיה.

APPENDICE IV

THE LETTER ZAYN

לד) עאלת את ﬣ ﬥ , אמרה ﬤ ליה : רבון עלמא, ניחא קמך למברי בי
עלמא, דבי נטרין בניך שבת, דכתיב ﬣ זכור את יום השבת לקדשו. אמר לה :
לא אברי בך עלמא, דאנת אית בך קרבא, וחרבא דשננא, ורומחא דקרבא,
כגוונא דנון, מיד נפקת מקמיה.

APPENDICE V

THE LETTERS VAV AND HAY

לה) עאלת את ₃ ל אמרה קמיה:רבון עלמא, ניחא קמך למברי בי
עלמא, דאנא את משמך. אמר לה: ואו, אנת ₍₎ וה, די לכון ₎ דאתון אתוון
דשמי, דאתון ברזא דשמי, וחקיקין וגליפין בשמי, ולא אברי בכו עלמא.

APPENDICE VI

THE LETTERS DALETH AND GIMEL

לו) עאלת את ס) ד ל) ואת ח) גֿ, אמרו ט) אוף הכי, אמר י) אוף לון, די לכון
למהוי יא) דא עם דא, דהא מסכנין לא יתבטלון מן עלמא, וצריכין לגמול עמהון
טיבו. דל״ת איהו יב) מסכנא, גימ״ל יג) גמול לה טיבו, לא תתפרשון דא מן דא ודי
לכון למיזן דא לדין.

APPENDICE VII

THE LETTER BETH

לז) עאלת את בּ אמרה ליה: רבון עלמא, ניחא קמך למברי בי עלמא, דבי מברכאן לך לעילא ותתא. אמר לה קב״ה: הא ודאי בך אברי עלמא, ואת תהא שירותא למברי עלמא.

APPENDICE VIII

THE LETTER ALEPH

לח)   קיימא את 𝑧 **א** לא עאלת. אמר לה קב״ה: 𝑢 אל״ף, אל״ף, למה
לית אנת עאלת קמאי כשאר כל אתוון. אמרה קמיה: רבון עלמא, בגין 𝑝 דחמינא
כל אתוון נפקו מן קמך בלא תועלתא, מה אנא אעביד תמן. ותו, דהא *) יהיבתא
לאת בי״ת נבזבזא רברבא דא, ולא יאות למלכא עלאה, לאעברא נבזבזא 𝑝 דיהב
לעבדו ולמיהב לאחרא. אמר לה קב״ה: אל״ף אל״ף, אע״ג דאת בי״ת בה אברי
עלמא, את תהא 𝑝 ריש לכל אתוון, לית בי יחודא אלא בך. בך ישרון כל חושבנין,
וכל עובדי דעלמא, וכל יחודא, לא הוי אלא באת אל״ף.

Index

Index